The
Be WUCA!
Way

March. 2019

May WUCA! ♥ inspire you
to new achievements!
Wonderful to meet you!
~Kim

The
Be WUCA!
Way

The ART of getting along

Thank you for you

FRANK AND KIMBERLEE SPILLERS

Talents + Love!
You are Awesome.

BALBOA
PRESS
A DIVISION OF HAY HOUSE

Be ~ WUCA!.
Learn ~ Act ~ Teach

Balboa Press books may be ordered through booksellers or by contacting:

Balboa Press
A Division of Hay House
1663 Liberty Drive
Bloomington, IN 47403
www.balboapress.com
1-(877) 407-4847

Cover and Illustrations designed by T1 Visuals, Dennis Groff.

Because of the dynamic nature of the Internet, any web addresses or links contained in this book may have changed since publication and may no longer be valid. The views expressed in this work are solely those of the author and do not necessarily reflect the views of the publisher, and the publisher hereby disclaims any responsibility for them.

The author of this book does not dispense medical advice or prescribe the use of any technique as a form of treatment for physical, emotional, or medical problems without the advice of a physician, either directly or indirectly. The intent of the author is only to offer information of a general nature to help you in your quest for emotional and spiritual well-being. In the event you use any of the information in this book for yourself, which is your constitutional right, the author and the publisher assume no responsibility for your actions.

Printed in the United States of America

ISBN: 978-1-4525-6907-9 (sc)
ISBN: 978-1-4525-6909-3 (hc)
ISBN: 978-1-4525-6908-6 (e)

Library of Congress Control Number: 2013903038

Balboa Press rev. date: 3/6/2013

To God

and

to my wife, Kimberlee,

without whose support and patience, I would never have gotten to really know what becoming WUCA! would mean for a husband and how it truly makes life meaningful.

May WUCA! be used to make a difference.

*"This is My Commandment, that you love
one another as I have loved you."*

John 15:12

Table of Contents

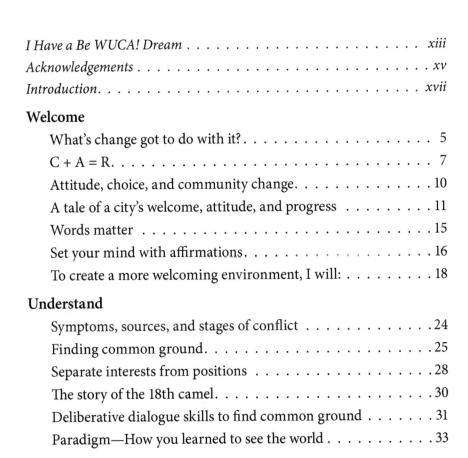

WUCA! in Action

Conclusion

I Have a Be WUCA! Dream

I have a dream that one day businesses, schools, churches, communities, and organizations will create an environment where all people and society will

Welcome, Understand, Comfort, and Appreciate!

When WUCA! happens, we will have loving families, happier employees, more volunteers, larger memberships, and growing populations.

When WUCA! happens, we will find more smiles on people, and dialogue more effectively between differing opinions. We will enjoy a respectful political landscape where our language lifts and sifts ideas and concepts, improving our country and world.

When WUCA! happens, environments change. Bullying will cease. Schools will produce passionate learners, churches will reflect the love they preach, and communities will engage all its citizens to benefit everyone.

When WUCA! happens, our workforce will support and strive

toward a common purpose, families grow together, and individuals understand and accept others.

When WUCA! happens, every customer, every employee, every volunteer, every spouse, every friend, every *person* will be accepted and respected.

I have a dream that when WUCA! happens in families, schools, churches, communities, businesses, and organizations, everyone will reflect a healthier attitude. People will talk **with** each other, not **about** each other, families will experience healing. Communities, growth and innovation. Churches, love. Businesses, prosperity. And individuals will rise to discover purpose and support others.

Be WUCA!

You will change the world.

Acknowledgements

To our many family members and friends who have supported our writing, we thank you. This project has taken much longer than we anticipated and we've cherished each word of encouragement you've shared.

Our artist/ illustrator, D.J. Groff. You've been a gem to bounce along with us on this ride. That we worship together, too, is awesome.

For the talents of our videographer, Ryan Paul Buck. Thanks for your skill, enthusiasm, and faith launching our visual products.

We've so appreciated the support of Balboa Press, especially to Adriane. You've been patient and supportive, calling us every week to see how the project was coming along—thanks for having faith in us to complete our first work. May we get to do it again!

We're so thankful to sister-in-law Mona Sears for your skillful ability to transcribe. You brought the original draft from audio to print and we are grateful.

To nephew, Nathaniel Sears, for product design ideas.

And for feedback on book content and cover to family, Melina Shouse and Jean Justin; and friends Chuck and Monica Farruggia, David Wilkinson, Cammy Brandt, Lydia Rothfusz, and Alice Johnson. Your caring, thoughtful insight helped shape the final form.

Thank you to C. Shawn Zanders, Rich Stoffers, Dr. Wendy Prigge, Mike Carter, Joel Davis, Bill Orlano, Margie Schwenk, Brent Jorth, and the staff and teachers of the schools that had the faith in us to teach their children the WUCA! way and provided a learning platform.

And to all of our students, from whom we have learned so much.

May you all make good choices.

Introduction

WUCA! Defined

It's Woo-ka

A positive, intentional choice every second of every day that creates an environment so the giver and receiver will welcome, understand, comfort, and appreciate.

Note: as you read the book, you'll see variations of the word forms. WUCA! is alive and its language flows, depending upon the setting and people.

WUCA! is an attitude. A lifestyle. It's your action of how you talk to, talk about, think about, and treat the people who cross your path every day. It is the environment that you create for you and others to live. We are excited to share our vision with you of a WUCA! world.

In WUCA!, *Welcome* is an attitude; a choice that can be broken into different meanings. "Welcome" can mean greeting or reception, the acknowledgement or expression of goodwill, or the state of being acceptable and accepted. When welcome happens, you choose to accept who you are and control how you think and act.

Live WUCA! You can influence who your friends are, the type of person that is attracted to you, and the impression you give to others. To feel (and look!) terrific, and act so people will choose to be around you, always extend an incredible amount of hospitality, whether you are at home, work, church, school, the gym, getting groceries, or walking down the street. Greet people enthusiastically with a big smile that projects welcome.

Understand means to be an active listener. Active listening means you hear not just the words a person speaks, but you seek to understand the underlying message being conveyed, making the speaker feel valued. You want others to know that you understand why they are, why they want what they want, and why their feelings matter. People will trust and respect you more readily when they know they are understood.

Live WUCA! Engage someone in conversation and truly listen to them. People who feel **understood** know that you have their best interest at heart. They will leave you feeling satisfied you heard their message.

Comfort is when you are comfortable knowing yourself, liking who you are, and are confident of the role you play in the lives of others and the world. When you are comfortable with yourself, you have identified your passion and purpose, have created a vision, and set goals for yourself.

Live WUCA! When you are comfortable, it transfers to others—they feel secure and relaxed the minute they come in contact with you. Your comfort allows you to help others discover their passion and purpose, helping them create a vision and set their own goals for the future because you know how. You live in physical well-being with low stress and peace of mind.

Appreciate is to express gratitude, recognizing that all people in your life have value and gifts to share. Acknowledge people for who they are and what they do for you. When you express gratitude for them, you will get back what you give.

Live WUCA! Everyone wants to feel appreciated! Be grateful. Show and tell people often how very much they make a difference in your life. Tell a person how much they mean to you and what their positive actions and words do to help you feel good about who you are. This simple, powerful choice to vocalize what we appreciate builds self-esteem.

When you are dealing with another person—a customer, co-worker, a classmate, a family member, someone in your church, a boss, an employee, or a stranger on an elevator or the street, treat them as important.

To **Welcome, Understand, Comfort, and Appreciate,** Be WUCA!

It's the ART of getting along.

Welcome

Welcome

---⊗⊗⊗---

It's all about attitude and the power of words

C AN YOU BRING TO MIND a person who makes you feel immediately at ease and comfortable? A good friend or a family member? Maybe it's someone who works at your local grocery or hardware store. Someone who always has a kind word to say? That warm feeling you receive is the "W" of WUCA! You feel welcome.

Our words and attitudes are completely intertwined so that one influences the other with each thought, word, and action.

We visited a church in a small town in Iowa one Sunday because we'd heard of its great music and strong message. The music and message were impressive, but what knocked our socks off was the welcome! We were greeted right inside the door by the son of the preaching minister with a big smile, strong handshake, greeting, "Glad you are here!" He led us to the woman in charge of welcoming guests, who greeted us just as warmly. She gave us a bulletin, a visitor's packet, gave us a quick visual tour of the lobby area, and then escorted us into the sanctuary, where worship was just beginning.

After the service, at least a dozen people surrounded us, assuring us they were thrilled to have us there and invited us to come with them to the park down the street for their summer potluck picnic. Well, in Iowa, we have potlucks all the time, but we were empty-handed, as we didn't know it was scheduled. No problem! Come anyway! So we did and had a marvelous time, staying with them for three hours and meeting dozens of people who went out of their way to share their food, table service, let us sit with their families, and told us all about the congregation. During the week, we received a card in the mail and a phone call hoping we'd return again. This church has made welcome an art form! This fabulous experience was a great lesson for us to look for newcomers in any setting and step out of our own comfort zone to make guests feel included and important.

When you want to build great relationships with other people, keep in mind that their ultimate goal is to feel glad. You want to create an environment so people feel important. Like this church did for us!

Ours is a blended family. When Frank and I were out visiting his daughter, son-in-law, and children in New York a few years ago, they made the most remarkable, noteworthy gesture. As a fellow avid reader, Frank's daughter knew that I loved the *Trixie Belden* series when I was growing up, having read each story dozens and dozens of times. Set in fictional Sleepyside-on-Hudson near Ossining, New York, one rainy afternoon during our trip, we all piled into their van and drove more than an hour downstate from their home. True-to-life from the books, we travelled up and down Glen Road as I snapped pictures of the houses and pond where the setting for my teen adventure mysteries took place. It was the first time I had met them and this trip touched me deeply and made me feel so very welcome. They went out of their way, very literally, to be kind to me. It was a lovely WUCA! experience I will remember the rest of my life.

Our attitudes are what draw people to us because of our tendency to be around other people with whom we feel great. When we have a positive attitude and look for good in all people and situations, acceptance and happiness often follow. Being a positive person means you are open and try your best to see the good in everything. You naturally attract others to you because you are hopeful, optimistic, and fun and people want to have the great time in life you do.

Attitude is actually a creative cycle that begins with your choice of thoughts. As you internalize ideas and become emotionally involved with your thoughts, you move your entire being—mind and body—into a new "vibration." Your conscious awareness of this vibration is referred to as "feeling." Your feelings are then expressed in actions or behaviors that produce various results in your life.

Another benefit of having a positive attitude is that positive things happen to you. When you decide you are going to be glad, glad you are. It's a choice. You *choose* to be glad. When you choose glad, things happen to you that will make you feel glad.

It is not just about having a "good feeling." Attitude and results are inseparable. Positive circumstances are always the result of a positive attitude. One is the cause, the other, the effect. Simply stated related to Being WUCA!, if you think in negative terms, you will get negative results. If you think in positive terms you will achieve positive, successful results. This is the essential core of being WUCA!

Try this experiment. Find a person with a bad attitude, stand beside them and just smile. Maintain your positive attitude. Think positive thoughts and believe in a positive outcome. The act of smiling, believing positively, and thinking positively will result in spreading your positive attitude. That other person will eventually smile because you shared yours. When you expose a positive attitude to others, it will spread to those around you.

What's change got to do with it?

We truly enjoy what we learn from Dr. Dr. Wayne Dyer. In his DVD, *The Power of Intention*, he tells the story of the message he leaves for people on his phone when he can't answer, "Hello, this is

Wayne, and I want to be happy. If your message is intended to bring me anything but happiness, then please call someone else."

Being happy is a choice. So is being a crap magnet.

In our workshops, one of our favorite diagrams asks this question: "Are you Happy?"

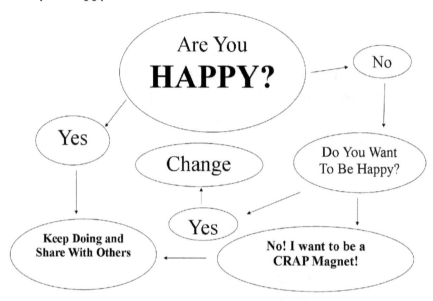

There are only two options to answer: "Yes, I am happy!" or "No, I am not happy."

If you answer the former, keep doing whatever you are doing.

If the answer is the latter, that leads to another question.

Do you want to be happy?

If the answer to that question is: "No, I do not want to be happy," then continue doing whatever you are doing.

But if your answer to the question is: "Yes! I want to be happy!" then you have to change something.

There's that word. Change.

No one or no thing can make you happy. If you aren't happy and you want to be, you must change something, otherwise you will remain the same. If you always do what you've always done, you always get what you've always got.

Untold people live their days with a poor attitude—you can likely name a few. Waking in the morning with the apparent goal not to be happy, they attract unhappiness. Their poor attitude attracts poor results and you could say that poor attitude people become "crap magnets" who look for the bad to happen in everything. And when bad happens, they say, "See! I told you! Nothing good ever happens." This becomes a self-fulfilling prophecy, blaming others for creating their unhappiness.

Which are you: a happiness magnet or a crap magnet? The choice is yours.

C + A = R

Just as you would use a map to take a trip, each morning when you get out of bed, you map your attitude throughout your day. Luckily, you get to drive your CAR!

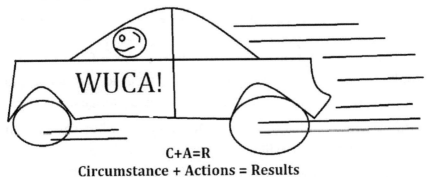

C+A=R
Circumstance + Actions = Results

"C" is *your circumstance;* whatever is happening at the moment. It could be at work, something done by the person near you, your spouse, something in the vehicle in front of you, or the weather around you.

"A" is *your action* to the circumstance. It could be that you did not get the promotion at work. A friend wants you to do something and you are not really sure it would be a good idea. You wake up and the first thing you do is stub your toe on something your spouse forgot to pick up. You are late for an appointment and the cars are moving *way* too slowly. And really? It's raining.

"R" is *your result*. When you identify the result you want, you can determine what action you need to take because however you act in any circumstance will determine your result. *You* have the ability to act in any way. It is *your* responsibility to determine *your* attitude to get the result of all of your circumstances.

So start with the result you want from a circumstance—many you can think about ahead so you'll know how to act when it happens. Choose your result and then act accordingly. Success is just a thought away.

Circumstance	+	Action	=	Result
_____		_____		_____
_____		_____		_____
_____		_____		_____

That person on the airplane next to you with a frown? If your result is to have a pleasant flight, no matter what, let your smile and friendliness be contagious to them to bring you *your* desire.

Look for ways you can add value to your job so when a promotion comes around again it will be obvious that *you* are the right choice.

It is not the fault of that slow-moving driver in front of you that you walked out of the house late. How will you drive *your* CAR in this instance?

And, of course, the rain. Last time we checked, there is only one who controls the weather.

When you take responsibility for your results, including your feelings, things start to happen. You get the results you want. You live life in a positive manner. You feel more in control because you take more control. Stop blaming others and other things for your emotions and feelings.

You cannot *make* people feel anything just like other people cannot *make* you feel anything. Eleanor Roosevelt put it this way, "No one can make you feel inferior without your consent."

An intentional survivor of three bestial concentration camps, including Auschwitz, internationally renowned psychiatrist Viktor E. Frankl once wrote, "Everything can be taken from a person but one thing: the last of human freedoms—to choose one's attitudes in any given set of circumstances, to choose one's own way."

Frankl is right. You could be faced with a thousand problems, over which many or most of them you have absolutely no control. However, there are always a few things of which you have complete control: your own attitude, words, and actions to a circumstance.

Attitude is actually a creative cycle—a composite of our thoughts, feelings, and actions. Our conscious mind controls feeling and ultimately dictates whether our feelings will be positive or negative by our choice of thoughts. Then our bodies display these choices through our actions and behaviors.

Ralph Waldo Emerson said it this way, "A person is what they think about all day long." Take a close look at your life and evaluate the results you are achieving in various areas. See if you are able to relate your attitude to your results.

As we internalize ideas or become emotionally involved with our thoughts, we create the second stage in forming an attitude: we move our entire being—mind and body—into a new "vibration." Our conscious awareness of this vibration is referred to as "feeling." Our feelings are then expressed in actions or behaviors that produce various results in our lives.

There are many things wrong in this world. Unfortunately, that is all some people are able to see. Those who view the world in this light are often unhappy and tend to be cynical. Usually, their life is one of lack and limitation and it almost appears as if they move from one bad experience to another. We know people who are like this and you likely do as well. It would appear they were born with a streak of bad luck following them ala Charlie Brown. These individuals tend to be quick to blame circumstances or other people for their problems rather than accepting responsibility for their life and attitude.

Conversely, there are others who are forever winning and living the good life. They are the real movers and shakers who make things happen. They seem to go from one major accomplishment to another. They're in control of their life; they know where they are going and know they will get there. Their wins are a matter of choice.

You can experience that kind of life as well; you only need to decide. Making that simple decision is the first step to a new life. Dorothea Brand once said, "Act as if it were impossible to fail." We challenge you to do so. By simply becoming aware that you can choose your thoughts each and every second of every day, you will change your entire outlook. You have the power to choose an abundant life, no matter your circumstances. That active choice will allow other positive people and opportunities to be attracted into your life. Step in to experience all the wonderful things the universe has in store for you. Start today, work on your attitude, and welcome the abundant life you were meant to lead. Remember: Circumstance + Actions = Results.

How will you drive your CAR?

Attitude, choice, and community change

We often seem to act with a "throw the bums out" mentality. We fire people when we don't like the environment. We throw out the volunteer when they do something we don't like and the activity is not going the way we think it should. We don't like the way things are so we want *someone else* to change the circumstances.

We proclaim, "We need change and we need it now!! I don't

like what is happening to me!" So we vote for people who promise us change. We hire people with different experiences to change our environment. We select people to lead us in organizations so *we* won't have to do the job.

But then we complain about the change we demanded. That we wanted. We say, "We can't do this" or "We can't do that" because **WE HAVE NEVER DONE IT THAT WAY BEFORE!!**

Or maybe like these thoughts:

The change didn't turn out the way I thought it was going to turn out.

Even though the change is for the better, it is not for the better for me and my situation.

The environment changed, but our circumstances did not. I am no better off now than I was before the change happened.

Is this what we hear in each political cycle? Could the problem be that *we* are the ones who need to change and we don't want to? That we really actually *like* things just the way they are because they are familiar, even if we complain? Even if someone that we vote into an office says they will change policies, processes, what's familiar to us? Then, if they actually do make changes, we say, "NO! We don't want to do that! It's really not what we want!"

A tale of a city's welcome, attitude, and progress

When Frank worked for a state department of economic development, he was part of a flood recovery team in a small community.

The town had spent several years planning, funding, and building a golf course. The night before the ribbon-cutting at the golf course, a huge flood came through the middle of town, destroying half the brand-new course, some buildings, parks, a trailer court, and a business. Thankfully, nobody was hurt.

He facilitated a town hall meeting with about 300 people in the school auditorium and tried to get them to plan and prioritize projects, but nobody would talk to anyone else.

After two hours, he sent everyone home and called for a meeting in the next couple weeks.

In the meantime, he went to the state historian. He explained the situation, wondering if the historian could shed some light on the town's history and current attitude.

"Frank," he said, "I know exactly the community you are talking about and why they are acting the way they are acting. 100 years ago..."

"Excuse me?" Frank interrupted.

"Yes," the historian continued. "100 years ago, the people in that town gave an award to the neighbor who hated his neighbor the most. That's why they won't talk to each other."

Armed with this information, he returned to the community at the town hall meeting two weeks later and told the story.

"So," Frank explains, "here you are a town of people who, for many years, woke up on New Year's Day declaring 'I'm going to win that award this year' and then acted accordingly. The competition was to determine how much more you could hate your neighbor than anybody else.

"The look on people's faces was amazing. They turned to one another and said things like, 'I wondered why my grandpa wouldn't let me play with you.' and 'Now I know why we didn't sit near you at school.'

"Though the competition died out, the culture remained. The town lived for more than a century with the attitude and culture of hating their neighbor. 100 years of progress stifled because of a contest and no one knew why."

The great thing is that once they heard the story at that meeting, they immediately were able to change their attitudes and set to work at once to rebuild their beautiful town.

In 25 years of career community development, Frank has found a consistent presence of non-WUCA! leaders. Commonly called the "old guard," or the "good ol' boys," they are typically very much ingrained in area tradition. They use the same approaches over and over again, often squelching new ideas, participation, and voices in decision making.

Communities and organizations with these gatekeepers still in place wonder why their communities are not growing. It is because, as Einstein put it, "the problems we face today cannot be solved at the same level of thinking you were at when you created them."

WUCA!-led communities are more open-minded, approachable, tend to have more newcomers, and they allow new people to make new ideas happen. Studies show U.S. state populations seeing growth have a higher percentage of newcomers than native-borns.

Another community where Frank worked told about a person who had moved to that community within the last two years. With three children enrolled in the district, she was at a school board meeting, and stood up to share her opinions on the issue at hand.

When she sat down, the lady next to her turned and told her that she had no right to talk at this meeting. The shocked woman asked why not. The woman replied that "she hadn't lived here long enough." Though she had children in the school, she'd only lived in the community a brief amount of time which, apparently, equaled her value and ability to contribute. In our town, we know people who moved to our community 30 years ago who still don't feel they belong because their grandparents aren't buried in the local cemetery.

As a leader, you need to look at your policies. Are they welcoming? As communities, counties, and states, do you allow newcomers to move in and do you embrace them? Yes, leaders love it when new companies come to town. There's a ribbon-cutting for a new business, a rousing welcome to all the new people to town, then, in a month, the excitement dies down and the new people that the community was excited about become "those" new people with all those "strange" new ideas. Or sometimes you hear comments when they become successful, they must have done something "wrong" and "underhanded" to gain that accomplishment. Communities, and people in general, have a habit of trying to pull successful people down to their level because there is a tendency to not like people who are doing better than they are because they have such low self-esteem.

Really, we often only like change if the change doesn't affect us.

The result is that the future remains the same because people often refuse to take their role as responsible citizens to make change that is necessary. It's hard work. It is messy. It requires talking to people. It requires acknowledging the world is not as black and white as we thought. Change requires slogging through the "gray" of an issue to see it through the eyes of another's experience. Change requires that we may have to give up our way and do it someone else's.

Remember that for every result that you want, there is a certain way of thinking, believing, and acting. You can change without improving, but you cannot improve without changing.

For a number of years, we've been very intentional about using words in conversation and in writing that are phrased positively, or at least as positively as possible. It's a *lot* of work at first, but with practice, it becomes so natural, positive phrases jump right out of your mouth!

Because words matter to your attitude and how you come across to others, try these phrases and see how they fit what you want to say. There have to be hundreds, maybe thousands more, so make your point to lead you and people you talk to feel better, think differently about what you've said, and maybe get a giggle that will affect the result of the conversation. Coin your own!

Words matter

NEGATIVE Emotion/Expression		TRANSFERS INTO POSITIVE Emotion/Expression
I don't ever want to lose you	to	I always want to keep you.
Never forget	to	Always remember
Don't want to miss	to	Be sure to see/attend
You can't do this until	to	When you do this, you can do this
angry	to	I try to see their point of view
anxious	to	expectant
depressed	to	on the road to a turn-around
destroyed	to	a change in course
that stinks	to	that's a little aromatic!
disappointed	to	what's important to learn?
disruptive	to	creative
embarrassed	to	stimulated
exhausted	to	recharging
failure	to	learning
frightened	to	inquiring
frustrated	to	challenged
furious	to	passionate
humiliated	to	learning moment
hurt	to	I will feel better soon
I hate	to	I prefer

impatient	to	anticipation
insecure	to	questioning
irritated	to	ruffled
lazy	to	storing energy
lonely	to	temporarily on my own
lost	to	searching
nervous	to	energized
overloaded	to	stretching
overwhelmed	to	challenged by many opportunities
overwhelmed	to	enjoying lots of variety in life
rejected	to	there's something better for me
sick	to	I'm being cleansed and healed
stressed	to	blessed

Set your mind with affirmations

Positive phrasing doesn't apply only to other people; it applies to us, too. We need to have our own bucket filled and sometimes we're the best—or only- ones around to do it.

The best way to change your mindset is with affirmations. We will talk more about how affirmations help you achieve your goals in the *Comfort* chapter, but for now, using affirmations is a great way to set your attitude.

It might feel different at first, but the more you do this the more comfortable you will be at telling yourself that you are a great person. Think of it this way: if you don't give yourself compliments, who will?

Here is the exercise to do. Go to a mirror whenever it suits you—first thing when you get up is great. Look yourself right in the eyes and say some or all of these statements out loud and add your own:

> » I am a winner!
> » I am the best friend I have.
> » I have the ability to handle all things.
> » I am capable.
> » I am smart!
> » I deserve to love and to be loved.
> » I am a skillful and artistic person.
> » I can show others a good example.
> » I am responsible for my own feelings.
> » I deserve to have my rights recognized.
> » I am a deserving human being.
> » I deserve to enjoy the fruits of my labor.
> » I deserve to be rewarded for what I do.
> » I love myself for who I am.
> » I am able to handle any problem I face.
> » I have the right to feel the way I do.
> » My family will benefit from me relaxing more.
> » Beautiful things happen often in my life.
> » I experience the excitement of growth daily.
> » I am working toward the blessing of change.
> » Taking risks is the path to growth.
> » I grow in love daily.
> » I am a rich treasure ready to be found.
> » God does not make junk.

- » I am confident.
- » My possibilities are endless.
- » I can handle all changes that come my way.
- » I can handle everything to comes to my life.
- » I am incredible!
- » I am the BEST person for the work ahead.
- » I am beautiful/handsome.
- » I am a champion!
- » I am PROUD of ME!
- » I love it when I stand up for myself in a respectful, thoughtful way.

If you want things to be different in your world, *you* have to have change. *You* have to let new things happen. *You* need to *act* the change that you wish to happen. *You* need to consider new ideas, maybe from new people.

- » Don't react to a circumstance. Be proactive.
- » When you act, choose your words and actions wisely.
- » Adjust your attitude.
- » Drive your CAR.
- » Be welcoming.

TO CREATE A MORE WELCOMING ENVIRONMENT, I WILL:

IN MY BUSINESS

_____

_____

IN MY WORKPLACE

_____

_____

IN MY CHURCH

_____

_____

IN MY FAMILY

_____

_____

IN MY SCHOOL

_____

_____

IN MY COMMUNITY

_____

_____

IN MY ORGANIZATION

_____

_____

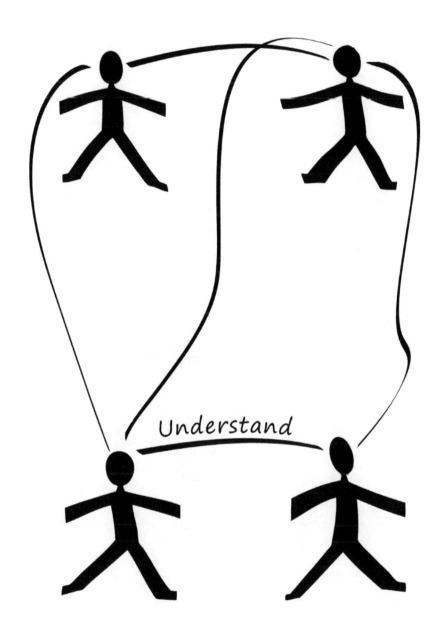

Understand

It's all about listening.

PEOPLE HAVE DIFFERENT BACKGROUNDS, DIFFERENT experiences, and different perceptions of the world. No two people ever see the same thing in the same way. They might come to agree on what they do see but they will have different paths to the agreement based upon the experiences of life they brought with them.

To fully understand another, to build a relationship with them, here's a simple rule of thumb: you have to understand how and why a person learns and becomes who they are.

In fact, if political leaders and countries follow this simple rule, there would be fewer wars, people would engage in the political process in greater numbers, and the health of nations would improve.

There are ways you can understand another's point of view and not agree with them. Love them as an individual but not condone what they do. You do not know what they have gone through or how they have grown up in this world.

In Stephen Covey's *The Seven Habits of Highly Effective People,* he urges "seek first to understand, then to be understood." Find out why a person thinks the way they do from what is or has happened in their life.

Every day, we're faced with issues where two sides are a snap to find. It's easy to see the pro and con. The right and wrong. Countries, states, cities, communities, neighborhoods, politicians, organizations, churches, businesses, families, and many other places where people come together to address issues face the same roadblock: "If they would just do it my way, the world would be so much better!" The problem with that mentality is that every other person likely wants to do it their way, too!

Symptoms, sources, and stages of conflict

We belong to several groups dedicated to learning and democracy called the Iowa Partners in Learning; the Kettering Foundation, in Dayton, Ohio; and the National Coalition for Dialogue and Deliberation.

The Kettering Foundation seeks to discover what it takes for democracy to work as it should. Through Partners, our Iowa work seeks to understand people, their motivations, and to address the "question behind the question" present in nearly all issues people could discuss through a marvelous process called *deliberative dialogue*. We've held and been a part of hundreds of these dialogues around the United States. We continue to be amazed at the depth and thoughtful insight each dialogue reveals showing our similarities are stronger than our differences when we listen to one another's stories.

Deliberative dialogue is values-based. It can be held on any topic from local community to international issues—economic and land development, healthcare, financial security, bullying, immigration, the role of the U.S. in the world, children, schools, and violence, to name a few. The beauty is that you can hold a safe, civil discussion about the topic when you know how. The goal is not to just talk *about* an issue, but to talk *through* it. To take the time to see what's going on from the viewpoint of another and the issue's impact on their life. More on this in a bit.

Issues have easy-to-spot symptoms that include increased tensions, disagreements and complaints, and blaming, avoidance of others—drama! Sources of conflict may include:

» Misunderstandings or failures to communicate

» Differences in values and goals

» Differences in approaches to work

» Roles and responsibilities that seem to be at cross-purposes

» Lack of cooperation

» Authority or noncompliance

» Differences in the interpretation of rules, policies, or standards

» Failure to listen correctly

Finding common ground

Conflict can be thought of as differences in perspectives, which are inherent in every relationship. The diversity of perspectives within relationships helps generate new ideas and facilitate innovative, collaborative solutions. If it is managed wisely, conflict is an opportunity.

Effective people often see conflict as a source of vitality and an impetus for change. They recognize and accept disagreement. By doing so, they not only find ways to analyze the conflict but also to manage and resolve it.

Effective leaders have cultivated a safe and supportive organizational climate in which relationships are based on inclusivity, trust, and mutual respect. Only in a supportive environment can people feel safe to express differences of opinions, and work toward "win-win" solutions.

Listening is a skill that requires intentional development. Just as you needed to learn how to walk correctly, relationships require the skill to actively listen because much of the time when an issue arises, the problem on the surface usually has a problem behind it where the true issue lies.

Here are some questions to consider when identifying the problem behind the problem. Be sure to involve all affected parties in the dialogue.

Naming: What do you think is the problem? What bothers you?

Framing: What can/should we do about the problem?

Deliberating: If we do what you suggest, what do you think would happen?

What would be fair? Effective?

Why would we be better off? How would we be better off?

What is/are the downside(s)?

If there is/are a downside(s) would we change our minds? What different course could we pursue?

Acting: What would you and the affected parties be willing to do about the problem? What are you willing to give up to do what you want to do?

When you listen actively, and talk *through* how people feel, you listen with different types of statements: encouraging, restating, reflecting, and summarizing.

1. *Encouraging* conveys a listener's interest in the topic and keeps the speaker talking.

The result will encourage the speaker to continue sharing their thoughts and experiences. Use noncommittal words and a positive tone of voice. Phrases like these indicate you care what the speaker has to say: "I see." "Can you tell me more?" "That's interesting."

2. *Restating* shows that you are listening and understanding, and lets the speaker know you grasp the facts of what they are saying.

The result of active listening is restating the speaker's basic ideas, emphasizing the facts. Examples are "If I understand, your idea is…" or, "In other words, this is what happened…"

3. *Reflecting* shows you are listening and understanding.

The result is to reflect the speaker's basic feelings. "You feel that…" or "You seem pretty disturbed by this…"

4. *Summarizing* pulls together important ideas and facts to establish a basis for further discussion, review progress, and restates, reflects, and summarizes major ideas and feelings.

Examples of this are, "These seem to be the key ideas you have expressed…" or "As I understand it, you feel this way about the situation."

Another way that a person communicates is by their body language. It is not only what they say, it is also what they do when they say it. The total impact of a message breaks down like this:

» Seven percent of a message is delivered verbally—in words.

» 38 percent has vocal delivery through volume, pitch, rhythm, etc.

» 55 percent of a message comes through body movements—mostly facial expressions.

Staying aware of and understanding body language is essential, since it accounts for most of the impact of communication, and is often more believable than verbal communication. The key is: are the verbal and nonverbal messages in agreement?

While there are more similarities between cultures in body language than there are in verbal language, the differences can cause serious confusion. For instance, maintaining eye contact while answering a question of someone in authority is a sign of sincerity in North American white culture.

For persons from other cultures (e.g., Puerto Rican, or Vietnamese) to maintain eye contact under similar circumstances would be a sign of disrespect. Thus, a respectful Puerto Rican might be judged untrustworthy by a white North American.

In observing and listening well to nonverbal messages, we need to be aware of our assumptions and judgments, and check them out in neutral language with the person and let the parties educate us about their meanings. If the parties themselves do not share the same cultural heritage, be aware that they may be unsure, too.

Separate interests from positions

Interests are the needs, concerns, and values that motivate each person. They represent why a person wants something, and they get at underlying issues—the problem behind the problem.

Positions are the actions a person will take to meet their needs. A position represents the outcome a person wants.

The ability to separate interests from positions is key to resolving conflict for these reasons:

> » Focusing on positions often creates a competitive, even combative, struggle in which each party is determined to win.

» Separating interests from positions allows parties to focus on the underlying issues rather than dealing with ideological or situational reactions.

» When you focus on interests rather than positions, it increases communication and the possibility of agreement.

» Identifying interests requires taking a step in defining and analyzing the conflict. Such a step is necessary to reach a resolution.

Separate interests from position by changing your focus. Rather than thinking about winning the conflict, think about what needs, concerns, and values motivate your position. Why is the issue important to you? What do you hope to gain? What do you fear you might lose? Then clearly state your interests rather than your position and ask questions to elicit and clarify the other parties' interests, needs, concerns, and values that motivate their position. These techniques to understand another's view can satisfy all parties and reach a win-win solution.

Too often, we encounter gridlock and impasse. More challenging, but worth the effort it takes to discover it is to find an alternate solution—a third choice—to an issue. We know from our learning and experiences that there is a better way to find common ground on tough issues using deliberative dialogue, based on understanding values. When you try to understand why others act the way they do, you can work together to identify a positive outcome in a safe space where people can come together, talk through perspectives on issues, and find common ground.

Who knows? Maybe a traveler will show up on a camel that provides a third choice.

The story of the 18th camel

The story is told of a Middle Eastern traveler making his way on a long journey across the desert.

As he plodded steadily on his camel through the dry heat, he came upon an oasis. Approaching the desert spring, the traveler was surprised to find three brothers weeping profusely.

Through conversation with the mourning brothers, the traveler discovered their father had recently passed away. The source of the tears was the brothers' inability to satisfy their father's last wish.

The father had given strict instructions that the inheritance of his estate be divided in such a way that the oldest received one half, the second received one third, and the youngest received one ninth of the father's estate.

The brothers had successfully divided the rest of their father's property, but were unable to do so with the camels. The father had left them 17 camels, and, try as they may, the brothers could not distribute the camels according to father's wishes.

The traveler considered the dilemma and then offered the brothers a solution. He insisted they receive his camel as a gift. After much conversation and many attempts at refusal, the brothers relented to the traveler's demands and received the kindness of his gift.

With 18 camels, the brothers were able to properly divide the inheritance and satisfy their father's wishes. The older brother received one half of the herd and took his nine camels. The second brother received one third of the herd and took his six camels. The youngest brother received one ninth of the herd and took his two camels.

Surprisingly, nine camels plus six camels plus two camels equals 17 camels. With the inheritance properly distributed, the traveler was able to take his camel and continue on his journey.

Deliberative dialogue skills to find common ground

Whether in a family, church, business, organization or a government, an issue goes through stages. When an issue is emerging, those involved and affected perceive their choices and choose their sides in resolving the matter. The closer we keep people involved and include as many choices as possible, the issue is less disruptive.

If we move away from giving choices to those who are involved, taking away their voice and input, the issue becomes increasingly disruptive. People who do not know how an issue is decided and are not a part of the decision do not trust the outcome. The more disruptive the issue, the higher the cost that issue is to resolve in time, manpower, and/or money.

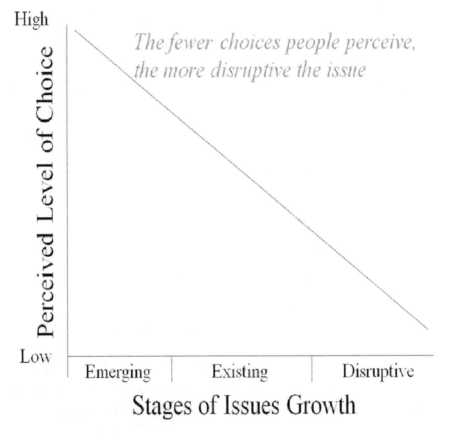

The fewer choices people perceive, the more disruptive the issue

High

Low

Perceived Level of Choice

Emerging · Existing · Disruptive

Stages of Issues Growth

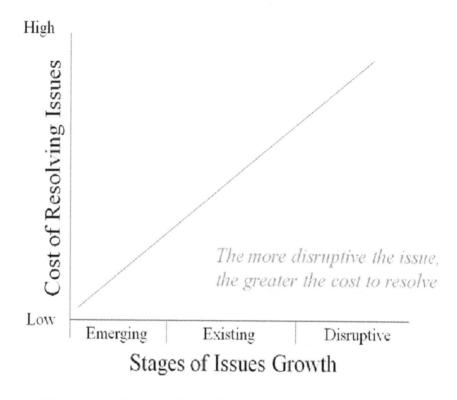

High

Cost of Resolving Issues

The more disruptive the issue, the greater the cost to resolve

Low

| Emerging | Existing | Disruptive |

Stages of Issues Growth

You can set the stage for building civil relationships and discover common ground with people. The next time you have an issue before you, use active listening and statements to reach a win-win solution:

» View people as problem-solvers.

» Separate the people from the problem.

» Be soft on the people, hard on the problem.

» Focus on interests, not on positions, or the bottom line.

» Help participants create multiple options for mutual gain.

» Use objective criteria.

» Reason and be open to reason; yield to principles, not pressure.

What solution do you have to offer to the desperate situations around you? Many times the answer is not either/or but in the third option, an option that you never would have found if you did not try and understand another's point of view. The solution might be right in front of you but you are too close to see it.

Paradigm—How you learned to see the world

To really understand another person you need to understand how your own filtering mechanism works.

Your filtering mechanism is your belief system of what you see or how you feel about a situation. Another word is paradigm. A paradigm is a belief that has been turned into a habit that has been programmed into you. It's how you perceive reality and why you act and live the way you do.

Each person is made up of the values with which they were raised and the accompanying sense of well-being. Our sense of well-being has three different components: the security we feel; the choices we feel we have; and the quality of life we perceive. These components rise from personal values we hold. If any one of these components is threatened, our sense of well-being is out of balance. When our sense of well-being is out of balance, we cannot move forward. We have to make sure as we build up people, they feel secure, they feel they have choices, and they feel their quality of life is intact.

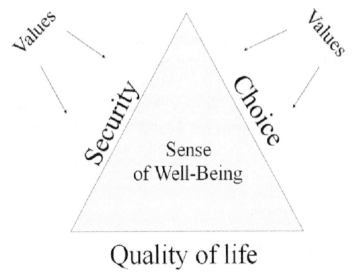

A paradigm is like railroad tracks: it creates a set direction for how you see the world. Everything you see, everything you do, everything you perceive of other people and situations is filtered through your paradigm. It becomes your reality.

In order to understand how another person perceives reality, you have to understand how they grew up; their culture. You have to understand their personality and their current situation.

You are a computer

For you computer types, here's a formula similar to driving your CAR, with a tech twist. All you have to do is insert the variable you want to change.

Your Body + Your Brain + Your Beliefs and Habits =
Your Results

You are constantly thinking. Your thoughts produce your actions which, in turn, become habits. What you think, what you believe, and what you do then programs your body, just as you would program a computer.

Your body is your computer hardware; your brain is your operating system—a Mac or a PC. Your beliefs and habits are the software you use to program your system. The system you have is only programmed to do what you tell it to do. You do not let anything into your "computer" unless you allow access because of your willingness to believe some outside external force such as other people's thoughts, actions, and opinions. If you want to change something about yourself, you have to change your programming—the software in your mind's storage systems.

As you know, you have two minds: conscious and subconscious.

Your conscious mind:

»   accepts or rejects any idea or goal.

» imagines and decides what you want to achieve.

» determines what actions you need to take.

» evaluates your goals and dreams and causes you to get excited about them.

» gets you to take action for a short period of time.

Your subconscious mind:

» controls 96 percent of all your decisions in your emotions, perceptions, and behaviors.

» controls all of your life's supporting systems.

» cannot tell the real from the imagined.

» immediately will act upon any idea impressed upon it.

» takes time to change something about us if we do not maintain our focus on our change.

» wants immediate results and when we don't see any change, we give up and tell ourselves that this stuff does not work.

You have to persist in the changes you want to make to be successful. You have to reprogram your computer to start living the change. When you put emotion into your change, you are 35 percent more effective in accomplishing your change. In fact, your emotional mind will hijack your logical mind to move you toward whatever and wherever you have emotion attached. As your subconscious mind always moves toward your thinking, keep focused on the change and persist until you are successful.

Who paints your canvas?

In his book, *Orbiting the Giant Hairball*, Gordon MacKenzie writes about everyone entering this world the same way, with a masterpiece to paint.

"In your mind, conjure an image of the Mona Lisa. Visualize that masterpiece's subtleties of hue and tone as clearly as you can.

Next, shift to the image of paint-by-numbers Mona Lisa. Envision the flat, raw colors meeting hard-edged, one against the other.

Now, let me relate a fantasy about masterpieces, paint-by-numbers and you. It goes like this:

Before you were born, God came to you and said:

"Hi, there!! I just dropped by to wish you luck and to assure you that you and I will be meeting again soon before you know it.

You're heading out on an adventure that will be filled with fascinating experiences. I was wondering, while you're over there on the other side, would you do me a favor?"

"Sure!" you chirp.

"Would you take this artist's canvas with you and paint a masterpiece for me? I'd really appreciate that."

Beaming, God hands you a pristine canvas. You roll it up, tuck it under your arm and head off on your journey.

Your birth is just as God had predicted, and when you come out of the tunnel into the bright room, some doctor or nurse looks down at you in amazement and gasps: "Look! The little kid's carrying a rolled-up artist's canvas!"

Knowing that you do not yet have the skills to do anything meaningful with your canvas, the big people take it away from you and give it to society for safekeeping until you have acquired the prescribed skills to requisite to the canvas's return. While society is holding this property of yours, it cannot resist the temptation to unroll the canvas and draw pale blue lines and little blue numbers all over its virgin surface.

Eventually, the canvas is returned to you, its rightful owner. However, it now carries the implied message that if you will paint inside the blue lines and follow the instructions of the little blue numbers your life will be a masterpiece.

And that is a lie.

You have a masterpiece inside you. One unlike any that has ever been created, or ever will be.

And remember: If you go to your grave without painting your masterpiece, it will not get painted. No one else can paint it.

Only you!"

Our early beliefs are formed through others

Do you remember what it was like when you were a kid? When you believed that you could be anything you wanted to be when you grew up? When you believed you could do anything and that anything was possible?

You could be a policeman or woman, a doctor, an astronaut.

You didn't have any doubts. You didn't have any judgments. You didn't see all the reasons "why not." You just saw the "What if?"

Do you still believe that you can be anything you want and have everything you daydream about?

Why not? What happened? Why don't we still believe money grows on trees? Why don't we still believe that we can have it all? Why don't we still believe that we are worthy enough? Why do we see all the reasons why it won't work, or why we can't do it, or why it's not possible?

It's not your fault that you believe this way. Here's why.

As we've lived life, our beliefs changed. Other people told us that

XYZ isn't possible. They told us that we have to work hard and life is a struggle. We aren't good enough. Or smart enough Or attractive enough. Or have enough money.

At first, we didn't believe them. We were still kids at heart. We thought we could have it all.

But then we tried something and failed.

And the more we tried—or saw others try and fail—we started adopting those beliefs as truths or facts. Through the years, they've become our beliefs. We started saying and believing: I'm not good enough. I'm not smart enough. Nothing ever works out for me. Other people are just lucky. Life is hard.

The list goes on.

Well, we're here to tell you that's not the truth. That's not who you are. That's not what life is about. Those are other people's old, worn-out, self-sabotaging beliefs. So don't buy into the negative of other people.

It's not your fault this voice got in your head. But it is your fault if you allow the voice to continue to be a barrier to your dreams.

C + A = R   Drive your CAR where *you* want it to go.

Every action you take and decision you make is a result of your beliefs. When you have positive beliefs in place, you will take actions and make decisions to allow you to live a life of freedom, happiness, fulfillment, and joy.

A child is born with certain traits: the color of eyes, the color of hair. If it's going to stay in or fall out later. If it's going to turn gray. Whether the skin will be freckled—whatever. Myriad possibilities are the things of your DNA.

As for us, we believe in God. We believe that God made us all the same way, originating from the same source. We are all made of the same energy. However, there are certain parts of us that aren't formed while we're a piece of energy. It is that blank canvas that starts to be painted at the moment of birth.

Many people holding brushes will put paint on your canvas. They will paint a picture the way they think the world really is, and the way they want you to be seen. The only problem is that it might not match who you really are.

This concept drawing, adapted from Bob Proctor, illustrates how we come into this world as an open container ready to be programmed and filled up. When we are born, other people start pouring in thoughts, ideas, visions; programming us through the way *they* feel, see, hear, smell, and taste.

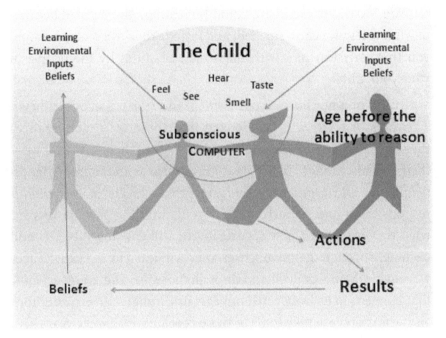

Think back to your first thought. How old were you when you have your first memory? Preschool? Three or four? Earlier? Later?

If we all come into this world at the age of zero, and don't remember anything until we are three or four or older, what happened between birth and our first memory? We are learning! We are being taught. We are being told things. We are experimenting with how the world works; learning what result we get from doing things a certain way.

Why don't you remember? What were you learning and who was teaching you?

You don't remember because your ability to reason had not yet developed and you were operating on your subconscious programming. One day you're crawling around on the ground looking at worms and putting them in your mouth. Soon, because you have developed your ability to reason, you look at a worm and don't put it in your mouth. How did you learn? You heard from someone not to eat worms, plus worms don't taste good.

You learned because you could feel things. You learned because of what you saw, heard, smelled, and tasted. Your five senses brought you this early learning with major contributions by the people in your young life.

Think of a newborn—your own, grandbabies, nieces, nephews, a friend's. Anyone who has looked into those little faces realizes they have no sense of reasoning at this stage of their lives and *we*— their parents, grandparents, great-grands, aunts and uncles, friends, neighbors, and especially childcare providers– have *tremendous* responsibility and opportunity for programming their brains for what they learn, and how secure, loved, and trusting they feel and become. Through their five senses, they will learn by the experiences we provide them—or not—and through those they initiate. *Everything* that happens to us from birth impacts us through our surroundings and what people supply to us in these precious, formative years.

As we grow older, our environmental inputs and ability to judge what happens to us and the way we allow the experiences to make us feel determines what we do, say, and, in large part, how we act. Because actions get results, we gain understanding from the results of our actions.

Our brains think, "If I do *this*, my result is *this*. I like the result I'm getting. I choose to do this again because this action makes me feel good."

For example, if you feel a hot stove, it burns your hand and hurts; therefore, you believe hot burners will burn you and it hurts. Or, as a child, if I hug my Mom or Dad and they hug me back, it reinforces my thoughts and actions. I like the result of my action because it makes me feel good, and so I repeat and include it in my personal belief system: hugging Mom and Dad is good! This is a large part of our early training when our personalities are formed.

A few years down the road, our experimenting changes because we have learned and can now reason. Now grown up, we look at a child and teach this conscious thought to them: "Don't put that in your mouth because it does not belong there!"

Now let's look at energy and how it creates the environment that creates you.

Vibration cloud

More than likely, you've had an experience trigger a memory, like visiting someone's home, walking into the kitchen, and smelling something that made you feel immediately comfortable because you felt secure. Sometimes just picturing a scene brings a flood of memories, tuned in by our senses. "Where have I smelled it? That smells like home."

Well, hopefully that's the good feeling you receive. Your feeling depends on your programming.

Maybe someone once hit you who was wearing green, so you avoid people who wear green because that color triggers fear in you. Maybe you instantly don't like someone because they remind you of a poor memory. Or you'll have an instant opinion of someone and make a judgment without even giving them a chance.

Our bodies live in a big, busy, complex world of thoughts, actions, beliefs, chemicals, and electrical energy. It is our response, thoughts, and actions to what is happening in our environment that determines who we are and what happens to us.

Here's how. We call it a "vibration cloud."

When something happens in our environment, we experience it through any of our five senses. As our senses filter through our conscious mind, we use our ability to reason and judge our environmental inputs to influence what we do. The mind then affects our body through our cells, releasing a multitude of proteins in our bodies. We determine what the experience means and if we accept it or not in our minds.

Our cells and bodies create energy from each thought, action, or experience that happens to us. As our emotions enter, energy intensifies. This energy sends a vibration into the environment that attracts more of the actions or experiences of the same vibration and the cycle starts all over.

This is why "like attracts like" and "as you think you become." Your vibration cloud is all around you. It is constantly in motion through your thought and attitude vibrations that impact your health. In fact, it affects everything about you every single day.

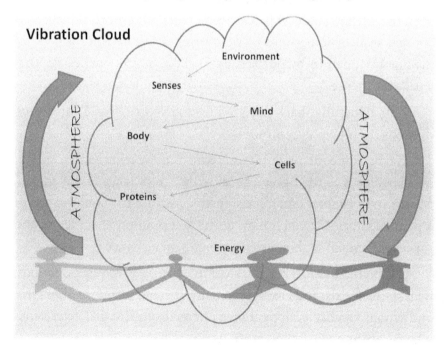

The great news is that you can affect the way you want your world to look and what attitude you will have. For example, if you wake up and decide it is going to be a bad day, your experiences line up to prove you right. But if you say "It's going to be a great day!" you look for things that will make it great.

No matter what you do during the day, at any given time, you are effecting, creating, and experiencing energy in your body.

Since everything is made of energy, everything you do, listen to, look at, creates energy. Things like:

- » Ideas you think about.
- » Songs you listen to and everything you hear.
- » Inventions are energy before they become structure.
- » Food is energy.
- » Magazines.
- » The books on your shelf.
- » Pictures and sayings on your walls.
- » Television shows and movies.
- » Everything you drink.
- » Your computer content is energy.
- » Thoughts.
- » Feelings.

So to make your day the way you want it, review your thoughts, look at what you put into your body, what you hang on your walls and create the environment that will give you the results that you desire. It's a cycle: your internal environment creates and reinforces your external environment, which, in turn, creates and reinforces your internal environment.

It begins within you! The world without will not change for you unless the world within changes.

What will you become today?

Keep in mind only four percent of what you do is a conscious thought, which means 96 percent of your actions, beliefs, and what you do are subconscious, because you have programmed yourself so well. How many of you grew up and said, "I'm not going to be like my mother?" How many of you are *just* like your mother, as in this story?

We have always done it this way!

A mother and daughter were preparing a roast for a family dinner. The daughter cut the ends off of the roast before putting it in the roaster, just as she was taught. She asked her mother, "why do we cut the ends off of the roast before we cook it?" "I am not sure," said the mother. "I guess it makes it taste better, but let's go ask Grandma."

So they went to ask Grandma. "Grandma?" asked the mother. "Why did you teach me to cut the ends off of the roast before cooking it?"

"Because it makes the roast taste better," responded Grandma. "Besides, that is the way my mother taught me. Let's go ask her."

So the three of them went to the person who started the tradition of cutting the ends off of the roast.

"Great-Grandmother why do you cut the ends off of the roast before you cook it? Does it make the roast taste better?"

"Heavens no," said Great-Grandmother. "I cut the ends off of the end of the roast because that is the only way I could get it to fit into the pan I used."

Sometimes it's helpful to look at the history of why we do things. Is it really necessary to continue some of the things we do or do we do them just because we are comfortable doing it that way? Do we do something just because we have always done it that way before?

You can change without improving, but you cannot improve without changing.

Do you know anyone who has changed their life because of the intentional choices they've made contrary to their upbringing or circumstances? We frequently hear stories of people who drive their CAR. They choose to break away from the environment they no longer want. Maybe they have a certain talent, like singing, and they must leave behind the familiar to create their own destiny. Sometimes people bravely choose to leave abusive situations to find a better way to live. They say, "I'm going to change my environment and I'm going to change the way I act to my environment. I'm outta here to find a new way to live!"

Maybe it's you. You want more. You have a burning desire to live differently than you are living. It takes conscious thought and commitment to change a view of the world. It requires constant, diligent, it's-in-your-heart-and-gut passion to change.

The biggest gap in growth is the gap between knowing and doing. In other words, you cannot grow if you do not do something toward it.

To discover the path in front of you, you have to start moving.

Understanding another person and understanding yourself takes much self-reflection. It takes asking questions and really listening to what is said by the other person.

The important point is to not jump to conclusions and form your opinion right away. Listening and seeking information are the steps to understand another. Become open-minded. Develop the skill to listen actively. Listen to understand.

What solution do you have to offer to the desperate situations around you? The solution might be right in front of you, but you may be too close to see it. Many times direction is not either/or, but lies in a third option, one that you never would have found if you did not try to understand another's point of view.

Blaming others is so easy to do. That way you don't have to take responsibility for your circumstances. You just point your finger and say, "if it wasn't for what they did, I would be so much better."

To see an issue from another person's point of view, you must work to understand why they have the position they do. What experiences have caused them to have that specific opinion?

Create your environment by adjusting your attitude and the energy you allow into your body.

Are you riding on the 18th camel?

Ask first what's happening with someone else.

Search to find the why.

Listen actively.

Be understanding.

To create a more understanding environment, I will:

IN MY BUSINESS

_____

_____

IN MY WORKPLACE

_____

_____

IN MY CHURCH

_____

_____

IN MY FAMILY

_____

_____

IN MY SCHOOL

_____

_____

IN MY COMMUNITY

_____

_____

IN MY ORGANIZATION

_____

_____

Comfort

Comfort

———— ⦿ ————

It's all about identifying your passion, purpose, vision, and goals.

Our Deepest Fear

Our deepest fear is not that we are inadequate. Our deepest fear is that we are powerful beyond measure. It is our light, not our darkness that most frightens us. We ask ourselves, 'Who am I to be brilliant, gorgeous, talented, fabulous?' Actually, who are you not to be? You are a child of God. Your playing small does not serve the world. There's nothing enlightened about shrinking so that other people won't feel insecure around you. We are all meant to shine, as children do. We were born to make manifest the glory of God that is within us. It's not just in some of us; it's in everyone. And as we let our own light shine, we unconsciously give other people permission to do the same. As we're liberated from our own fear, our presence automatically liberates others.
—*Marianne Williamson*

COMFORT IS KNOWING YOURSELF. IT's being comfortable in your own skin with who you are and knowing the values that guide your life. It is doing what you were created to do.

Some people are afraid to become what they dream of being. You feel scared or you don't deserve to have what you dream. Maybe you've heard "Dreams are for kids!" or "You need to stop dreaming and live in the real world!"

What if you are not living in the real world because you are not living your dreams?

We define success as "doing what you were created to do."

American motivational author, Alfred Montapert, once said, "To accomplish great things we must first dream, then visualize, then plan...believe...act!"

Visualize yourself in 10 years. Whether you do something different than you are now or not, 10 years from now will happen. The choice you have to make immediately is that you can discover your purpose now and live it in the next 10 years or you can wait the same 10 years, look back and ask, "Why am I still doing what I am doing?"

Living your passion, discovering your purpose, creating your vision, and striving toward achieving your goals is the most fulfilling life experience you can have. When you do what you were created to do and live your purpose, you will also help other people discover and live theirs.

Here's how we describe the four important components to being comfortable with yourself.

Passion is that burning desire deep within you to do that activity or work you love every chance you get. When a person cultivates their passion, they know exactly what they want. They think about this passion every day of their lives. They have a burning desire of exactly what they want to do, and that desire carries them over every obstacle as they pursue their goals.

Purpose is that feeling you are doing exactly what you were made to do. You GET to do. It gets people up in the morning and keeps them giving their very best all day long. It's the last thing that you want to do before dropping off to sleep at night. When you are on purpose, you are fulfilling a cycle for others to fulfill theirs.

When you are living your purpose, you manifest the glory of God that is within you.

Vision is the picture of the future we wish to create. It is a crystal-clear photograph of how we see our dreams becoming reality. Visions are very powerful forces that direct our mind and actions to achieve our dreams. "An actor's dreams are an insight to his greatness," said Charlie Chaplin. So dream big and be great!

Goals are mandatory, as humans are goal-seeking organisms. Everyone was built to have goals, giving you direction and a reason to live. Much has been written about when people retire from their careers, they lose direction in their life and age much more rapidly and sometimes die sooner just because they have lost their reason to exist.

Growth in your life must be intentional. You have to reach out and take the road you want to travel. Build the trail to success. Create an encouraging, goal-seeking environment.

Of course, success means different things to different people. For some it's starring in a movie. For others it's owning your own business, or getting a great job. It could be working at a zoo or with a veterinarian because you adore animals. Successful people are the ones who live their purpose, accomplish their dreams, and the goals they've set for themselves.

Thoreau said that if you want to be successful, you first need to identify your dream. Then you must think about it often and take active steps every day to move in the direction of your dream. Only then, after many days, weeks—and sometimes years—of focused effort, will success truly be yours.

You might be thinking, "Sure that only works for some people. But I have bills and worries about just making it through the day." Let's help you to figure the steps to find your success.

Clearly define your dream and you'll take a BIG step closer to becoming the person you're destined to be. You can do it!

Discover your passion

What are you doing when you feel really alive? Discovering what you are passionate about is the first step in revealing what you were put here on Earth to do.

Whether you are just beginning your career path, contemplating a new direction, or are well-established in your profession, you should feel passionate! Ready to take on the world, you know you are in the right place at the right time. Changing the status quo is your only agenda. Shaking it up and making the world a better place is your focus.

We equate real passion to a vigorous kind of enthusiasm you feel deep within you that isn't easy to explain or define. This burning desire propels you in a direction motivated by a force beyond your control. It's the inner excitement of being on the right path, doing what feels good to you, and what you know you were meant to do. The mere presence of passion within you is what you need to fulfill your dreams. That said, do keep in mind that changing attitudes, habits, and maybe career paths will take time, dedication, perseverance, intention, and action.

When you're enthusiastic, nothing seems difficult. When you have passion, you are willing to face the risks. You know you have the strength, smarts, and confidence to succeed. Enthusiasm carries you through and helps you rise above barriers to live out your passion. That's because you're answering your calling—the *you* who is doing the answering is the highest part of you, or the God within.

Think about working passionately at what you love. What are you doing? What are you feeling? Do you have sharp focus, clear vision of your future, total control and mastery over your work? A healthy body, and an exuberant attitude?

Are you doing those things? Are you living those feelings?

If you are not, you are not living your passion. Yet.

People will tell you that it is not feasible to live your passion. "I can't make money doing what I love. I don't have the time or I am too busy trying to make ends meet to do what I am passionate about."

This is resistance. Why would you make excuses not to do what you love?

Passion is God's way of pushing you in the direction He has prepared for you.

There is always a way to pursue your dreams.

How do people who are doing what you want to do do it? What do they do differently than you are doing?

Listen to your self-talk, your mind-chatter. Everything you tell yourself, someone taught you to think, telling you you can't do what you want. Look around and list all the people doing what you would love to do. Is your mind chatter in the way saying things like,

You have to do this to make a living?

You can't really make a living on what you love to do—no one can.

It is unrealistic to think that you can be happy working.

No one is really happy at their job—it's just a way to make a living.

It doesn't have to be that way. There are people living their passion. We are two of them.

Life is too short to try and just get by. We listen to other people, even those closest to us, much too often. Other people may have our best interest at heart, but usually talk from *their* experiences, not *ours*. They mean well, but they want to remain in *their* comfort zone and everyone else to stay there, also.

Other people can harm or scare you, creating horrific memories, but they cannot ruin your life without you giving them permission.

Step out; find what you are passionate about. If your spiritual life encourages you, pray that a way presents itself, and then go for it. Find an accountability coach to help you and start fresh with your life.

You will be a much better person for it and those who love you will appreciate the new you!

Finding your passion does not come overnight. Taking proactive steps you'll see a gradual increase in your enthusiasm. You will begin working with a newly-fired zeal which becomes contagious, attracting and motivating others who support you, as well. You will have consciously taken charge of your life and the fruits of prosperity will be in sight.

Find your passion and change your world. Here are some starter questions to get you going. These exercises will take time to truly discover who you are. Give yourself at least a day or weekend retreat—maybe more. What you learn about yourself will be very rewarding to plan your future. So grab your iPad, computer, or plain ol' yellow legal pad and your favorite beverage and spend some time getting to know *you*.

First, rate yourself between 1—5, with 5 being the highest, on each of the following statements.

_____ I recognize what I am good at doing.

_____ I fully utilize my most enjoyed skills and interests in my personal and professional life.

_____ My work furthers issues about which I care deeply.

_____ Through what I do with my life, I see myself making a difference in the world.

_____ I view my workdays with enthusiasm.

_____ I take necessary risks to live my philosophy.

_____ I feel a sense of meaning and purpose in my life.

_____ I have goals related to that purpose.

_____ I live my life now rather than hoping it will work out someday.

Total score, with 45 being the highest possible _____

Look at your score and the statements that you did not rate yourself as high as you want. Think about what would have made that statement a 5 instead of the score that you put.

Then take the next step.

Identify your passion, your first step toward creating the rest of your life.

Complete the following:

I am really good at _____

At work _____

At home _____

At church _____

At play _____

I am very excited when I am doing _____

At work _____

At home _____

At church _____

At play _____

I dream of doing _____

At work _____

At home _____

At church _____

At play _____

I care most deeply about this issue _____

At work _____

At home _____

At church _____

At play _____

Review what you have written on the lines above. Put them all together and finish this sentence: Even if I would not get paid a dime, I would:

_____

_____.

Bonnie Ware, a hospice nurse to people with fewer than 12 weeks to live, asked her patients what, if anything, they regretted as they look back over their lives. Every single one of them said: "I wish I'd had the courage to live a life true to myself, not the life others expected of me."

She continues, "This was the most common regret of all. When people realize that their life is almost over and look back clearly on it, it is easy to see how many dreams have gone unfulfilled. Most people had not honored even a half of their dreams and had to die knowing that it was due to choices they had made, or not made. Health brings a freedom very few realize, until they no longer have it."

Dr. Wayne Dyer puts it this way, "Don't die with the music still in you."

Identify your purpose

Have you ever wondered why you are here? Why you are in this place? Why you are with the people you are? Why you like to do some things more than others? What is your purpose?

Jack Canfield, in his bestseller, *The Success Principles, How to Get From Where You Are to Where You Want to Be,* lays out an easy way to create your own purpose statement. Put some thought into these questions and let's discover your individual purpose.

Step 1 Identify what makes you happy.

What are the things that you are most passionate about and bring you the most joy? Make as long a list as you'd like.

_____

_____

_____

When are the times you have felt the most joy? Think on all your various experiences in your life.

What has touched your heart deeply?

_____

_____

_____

What are the common elements?

_____

_____

_____

Step 2 Identify who you are.

List two of your most unique personal qualities, such as "I'm enthusiastic and creative."

_____

_____

_____

List one or two ways you enjoy expressing those qualities when interacting with others, such as, "I support and inspire people."

_____

_____

_____

Step 3 Describe your perfect world.

Assume the world is perfect right now. What does this world look like?

_____

_____

_____

How is everyone interacting with everyone else?

_____

_____

_____

Write your answer statement, in the present tense, describing the ultimate condition, the perfect world as you see it and feel it. Remember, a perfect world is a fun place to be! Examples: Everyone is freely expressing their own unique talents. Everyone is working in harmony. Everyone is expressing love.

_____

_____

_____

Step 4 Combine your responses into a single statement.

For example, Global Horizons' purpose statement is "*to use big picture visioning and passion to motivate and guide others to discover their unique talents to be involved in building the future. We do this by providing, creating, and teaching innovative processes that bring the best out of people to successfully move forward in a Be WUCA!(c) way to Welcome, Understand, Comfort, and Appreciate to build civility in the world.*"

Purpose is the *why* you do something. It is the statement you create to measure what you do to your individual purpose. The idea is to match what you do on a daily basis to what you were made to do. If you don't do the work to find out what your purpose is, you forfeit the right to complain about your life.

_____

_____

_____

What importance does purpose have to how we live?

Everything.

If you are living your purpose, what you were made to do, you will be successful! It is the "why" of "why were you created." It is the "why" you were given breath.

Purpose of Breath of Purpose

"And the Lord God formed man of the dust of the ground, and breathed into his nostrils the breath of life, and man became a living being." Genesis 2:7.

Have you ever witnessed someone dying? Watching him or her take their last breath of life?

Nothing changes except they don't breathe in any more. They exhale one last time.

I, Frank, was with my wife and brother-in-law in the room with their father, my father-in-law, during his last moments here on earth. It was a very peaceful death. In fact the nurse said that she has never seen anyone die this peacefully with end-stage COPD.

As we were surrounding him with love and giving him permission to go, we watched. I watched him breathe in and out, looking at the vacant stare in his eyes in his last hours of life, his labored breathing increasingly less. I looked at him to see if his chest would expand again, watching with anticipation, but praying that this was the end of his suffering. It was.

At his last moment of his life, he looked me in the eyes and breathed his last. An exhalation. He was finally at peace.

What does this have to do with the breath of life?

Everything!

When you are born—your first human action is to take a huge breath of air. That breath gets everything going. The sound of your cry, or maybe a scream, is a huge blessing and one of the happiest moments for a parent!

That breath is the foundation of moving, speaking, feeling, smelling, and is the basis of all that you learn. With that breath, life begins. Without that breath, life ends.

I believe God gives you that breath of life. God provides that breath as the Holy Spirit within you. I believe that breath is your proof that God exists within us and we are connected to God.

When my father-in-law exhaled for the last time, nothing changed. His body was still there, but there was no life. No movement. He didn't see or smell things. He didn't feel anything anymore. His life was gone but his body was still there.

We are using these shells we call bodies to live inspired lives. Dr. Wayne Dyer states that, "We are spiritual beings having a human experience." God knows when we have fulfilled His purpose on this Earth, and then He calls us home, leaving our shell.

It is up to us to discover that purpose and become aligned with it. Those who live with passion, full of life, and on purpose, are those who will hear when they are called home, *"Well done, good and faithful servant! You have been faithful with a few things; I will put you in charge of many things. Come and share your master's happiness!"*

Matthew 25:21

God blesses us with others, and puts others in our way to fulfill His purpose and the purpose he gave us to fulfill in our life.

He uses breath to accomplish that purpose. He gives us breath to allow Him to work through us. He gives breath to live in us. It is our responsibility to live that purpose, using the blessings that we have received to help others live their purpose. This is the true cycle of life.

"It was now about the sixth hour and darkness came over the whole land until the ninth hour, for the sun stopped shining. And the curtain of the temple was torn in two. Jesus called out with a loud voice, 'Father, into your hands I commit my Spirit.' When he had said this, he breathed his last."

Luke 23:44—46.

It was done. His purpose had been fulfilled.

What about you? Are you using your God-given shell that is full of life, full of spirit, breathing in and out God's energy? You are connected to life in a way in which you can flourish. I choose to live with the knowledge that God is with me, in me, and also in you. Are you living on purpose?

Create your vision

"Vision gives you the impulse to make the picture you own," said American speaker, Robert Collier.

Your vision is your ideal life. It is what you dream about and have pictured in your mind as an end result.

Stephen Covey's habit put it this way, "begin with the end in mind." In other words create the picture of the environment that would be created when you achieve all of your dreams.

You should actually have a written vision for everything. What are you doing in your dream job? Where are you living? What does your house look like? What does your spouse look like and how do they act toward you? Who are you helping? What does your environment smell like, taste like, and feel like? What sounds do you hear?

Describe what you see in detail. Color. Smells. Location. Whole, healthy body. Your home. Give it shingles and windows. Two- or four-door car. Income. Restored relationships. Be specific.

A contractor once told a story about a house that he was building for a woman who was blind. The plans were drawn and many visits between the two were had as the house was being constructed.

The time came for the final walk-through. The contractor thought that everything was perfect. He was very proud of the work he did. In fact he was so proud that he thought to himself that he could live in this house.

As the contractor and the woman were walking through the house, she noticed three very slight flaws. The flaws were so minute that a sighted person probably would have overlooked them. But this woman's picture was so focused and clear on exactly what she wanted, she found things out of place, not in her vision.

That is how clear and focused you want your vision to be. When you have a clear vision of where you are going and a burning desire that you are going to get there, nothing will stop you.

A vision that is shared between people can create excitement. It will create a common road for you and others to travel.

Your future will be created with or without you. You can either be an active participant or a spectator sitting on the sidelines living whatever comes along.

Great leaders have been known to be gifted with vision, able to create excitement about the vision and where you are going to end up.

When you get people behind a great vision, you will have an amazing time.

John F. Kennedy did this in the 1960s when he laid out his vision to the nation to go to the Moon by the end of the decade. He created a vision that people could support and be excited about so everyone took a part in achieving it and making it successful. NASA even had a huge picture of the Moon on the wall immediately inside the doors so that all employees and visitors would see the vision and keep it in front of them at all times.

If you see where you are going, you'll get there.

Establish your goals

When you have identified your passion, written your purpose statement, and created a vision for your future, it is time to take action to bring the picture to life.

Goals are your steppingstones to achieve your vision. Something happens within you when you write down each of your goals. This one step, establishing your goals and then working to achieve them, changes your life. It is the step-by-step process of reaching your vision.

That said, this does not happen overnight. You have to work at it. You have to act on your goals. You are telling your brain you have committed to a promise about getting to the end.

Many people are great at setting goals, but not quite the master at achieving them. Don't be discouraged, you're not alone. In fact, research has shown that by January 17, people who created a New Year's resolution have given up. Fortunately, you're not a lost cause, either. Breaking your goals down into a few key elements could be the difference between all talk and all action.

One way to remember these key elements is to think of your goals as SMART: Specific, Measurable, Attainable, Relevant, and Timely. Let's take a look at what each of these elements mean and how you can apply them to better set and reach your goals.

1. Specific

You're much more likely to achieve a goal if you get specific. Most people don't realize how vague their goals actually are.

Being specific will not only give you clarity of what's required, but it will also make it less daunting because you have a specific focal area.

2. Measurable

Establish concrete criteria so you can evaluate your progress as you go. Break your big goal down into small targets you can track.

For example if you want to start to test market your business idea, you could decide that you will tweet once a day on Twitter, or post a status update once a day on Facebook or LinkedIn. Now you've got a set item that you can add to your to-do list, just like you would any other task—and you can cross it off your list as "done." Your goal is now in action. And, as MarciaLee Sears says, "Done is good!"

3. Attainable

You want your goal to be a challenge, but also one that you truly believe is possible to achieve. Don't say you're going to write a book this summer if you know you've got engagements every other week and you don't have time set aside. Pick something reasonable that you can really see yourself achieving.

Can you see yourself writing 250 words a day or five pages a week? If you know you can do it, and you start meeting your quota, you'll notice that you'll gain momentum. Goals that once seemed out of your reach become attainable, and you'll grow and expand to match them.

4. Relevant

Are your goals relevant to and coincide with your purpose? Do your best to match them so that you reach your purpose most quickly. Stay on target!

5. Timely

Set a specific date for when you will achieve your goal. It will give you a sense of urgency and also help you keep things in perspective in real time. You will automatically move toward accomplishment. This way, you go from having a "someday" kind of plan to having a concrete guide for the months and years ahead.

Don't be afraid to adjust your goals as you move forward. The important thing is that you are moving toward your end.

The secret of success is persistent action. The secret of persistent action is a burning desire and clear vision of where you are going. Keep working toward your goal. You will hit it.

Affirmations to get you started

We become what we think about, so program your mind with the goals you want to achieve. Use your goal statements as affirmations to motivate yourself to achieve your desires.

Here are some simple steps you can take to help you achieve your goals.

1. Conceptualize. Make an affirmation for each of your goals on a 3 x 5 index card. Go through the set repeating and visualizing them at least three times a day—maybe the first thing when you get up, in the middle of the day for course correction, and around bedtime. Or print them on a piece of paper and laminate it to post around your house or workplace. Both, if you can. Carry them with you. You choose the method—the important thing is to remind yourself often.

2. Prioritize your statements from most to least important. It is better to work consistently and in-depth with a few affirmations than to occasionally repeat a lot of them.

3. Visualize. Close your eyes and visualize yourself experiencing what the affirmation describes, using your senses. See the scene as you would if you were looking out at it through your eyes, happening around you. Smell? Is there anything to taste in your new bakery you want to open? How do your new clothes feel? Post pictures of the things you want around your house or room. Include yourself in the picture.

4. Vocalize. If you are in a private place, read each affirmation out loud. Repeat your affirmations silently or out loud making sure to use time such as waiting in line, exercising, or sitting at a stoplight. Hear any sounds you might hear when you successfully achieve what your affirmation describes. Include other important people in your life congratulating you and telling you how pleased they are with your success.

Adding emotion with your affirmations will make them 35 percent more powerful and will lead you more quickly to the result you want. Think about how terrific you will feel when you have achieved your goal and let it fill you. For example, you can say over and over to yourself, "I feel healthy and attractive at my ideal weight of ___!" Feel the feelings and excitement when you achieve this success. The stronger the feeling, the more powerful the process becomes and the more quickly you will achieve your goals.

You can even record your affirmations and listen to them while you work, drive, or fall asleep.

When you are living your passion and you are on purpose, opportunities will unfold before you. Be prepared to act upon them. Consider if you are doing everything you can. Are you preparing yourself or are you just waiting?

Fully engage with what you are doing and give it all that you have with enthusiasm! Keep moving, be persistent, don't worry, and trust that you are doing exactly what you are supposed to be doing and you will create the future you dream about. It will happen; you have to keep moving.

Focus on your positive goals and concentrate on your affirmations for the future.

Will you experience failure? Most likely. People will probably tell you that you are crazy. Your dream will never happen. They will try and pull you down and not lift you up. Circumstances may surface that you did not see or plan.

When you fail, people will say, "I told you so." If you are successful, people might be jealous of your success and may try and pull you down to their level.

Will that be all right? YES!!

Growth takes place with learning, so when you fail you get back up, brush yourself off, look back and ask, "What did I learn?" Then move toward your vision. Again and again and again.

It doesn't matter how many times you fall or you get knocked down by others. What matters is how many times you get back up. Having passion behind your goals is feeling and knowing you are doing exactly what you were made to do and that you are on purpose.

Determining direction and purpose in your life will reduce the frustration of living day to day in a fog. It all happens for a reason. It is up to you to find it and live it.

We are not living as an independent person on this planet. We are all connected. What we do affects other people and events. When we live our purpose, we allow others to live out theirs.

When we have passion for what we do, purpose for why we are doing it, vision for where we are going, and goals to get there, we will live an inspired life. A life where we are comfortable.

Know yourself.

Help others know themselves.

Define purpose, passion, vision, goals.

Be comfortable.

TO CREATE A MORE COMFORTABLE ENVIRONMENT, I WILL:

IN MY BUSINESS

IN MY WORKPLACE

IN MY CHURCH

IN MY FAMILY

_____

_____

IN MY SCHOOL

_____

_____

IN MY COMMUNITY

_____

_____

IN MY ORGANIZATION

_____

_____

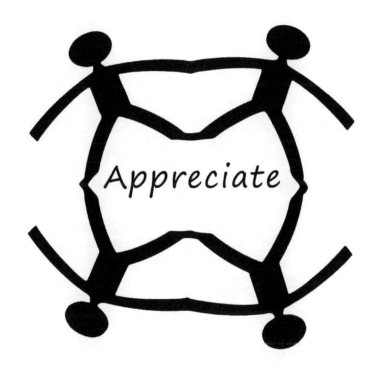

Appreciate

It's all about expressing gratitude

ONE OF THE EXERCISES IN the *comfortable* chapter encouraged you to describe your perfect world—how it would sound, what you would see, hear, taste, and smell. The picture you created is your own garden of paradise here in this life.

When we talk of appreciation, keep in mind a few things about gratitude.

First, gratitude is not the same as indebtedness. Indebtedness occurs when a person perceives that they are under an obligation to make some repayment of compensation for aid. The emotions lead to different actions. Indebtedness can motivate the recipient of the aid to avoid the person who has helped them, whereas gratitude can motivate the recipient to seek out their benefactor and to improve their relationship with them.

Next, gratitude serves to reinforce future behavior in people. For example, studies have found that employees want to be appreciated and recognized for a job well done more than they want more money.

In another study, regular patrons of a restaurant gave bigger tips when servers wrote "Thank you" on their checks.

When it comes to gifts, appreciation should be automatic, as gifts are not entitlements. Throughout the year, opportunities abound for generosity to family members, friends, organizations, charities. It is appropriate to express gratitude when gifted with money or a loaf of bread, a job interview, a party, or a kindness of some sort. Get out that pen and dash off a heartfelt thank-you to whomever gifted you. A phone call. An e-mail. *Some* form of communication to connect your appreciation that someone thought of you. Doing so encourages the giver to think more positively of you and be, perhaps, more likely to gift again.

And, of course, there is gratitude for the beauty of the world and what is taking place in your life that is right and good. Even in the midst of horrid circumstances, we can find beauty if we choose to name it. Viktor Frankl, survivor of the Auschwitz concentration camp wrote in *Man's Search for Meaning* of finding beauty in his food during his imprisonment in the fish head floating in his daily bowl of dirty water.

What's in your life that makes you overwhelmingly grateful? When you take just a few minutes each day to jot down things that make you thankful, you will feel better about yourself, have more energy and feel more alert. In less than 60 seconds a day, just by writing down those things for which you are grateful, you will instantly raise your emotional set point and feel happier.

Clean your window to the world

A couple moved into a new home in a new neighborhood. When the wife did the laundry and hung it outside, she looked out the window and saw the clothes that she just washed were still dirty.

She brought them back into the house and washed them a second time, hung them out to dry, but when she looked at them from the kitchen window again, the clothes were still dirty.

Thinking that the washing machine that came with the house was broken and not getting the clothes clean, she talked her husband into buying a new washer.

When she washed clothes in her new washing machine the next day, she again hung them out to dry, but when she looked out the window, they were still dirty.

Complaining to her husband that the clothes just are not getting clean it now must be something in the water.

Her husband looked out the kitchen window at the laundry, got a ladder out, washed the window and then had his wife look out at the laundry.

She exclaimed excitedly that now her laundry was clean.

The filter through which we look makes our world. When you look at the world through a filter of appreciation, you will see a brighter world with a brighter future.

Choose to appreciate the here and now.

Appreciation stops negative thoughts

"How do I stop my negative thoughts?" is a question we have been asked many times. If you have ever asked this question, then you will feel such enormous relief in knowing the answer, because it is so simple. How do you stop negative thoughts?

You show *appreciation* and plant *good* thoughts! Start every single day by being grateful for what you have. Visualize your goals, and put feelings to them as if you have already accomplished them. Believe that you are exactly where you should be and you are going in the direction that you should be going.

Think about starting a blessing/gratitude board. We have a whiteboard on our fridge and jot down blessings on it often so they are right in front of us as constant reminders of the abundance in our lives.

This simple act of expressing gratitude and looking at where you plan to go with your life is very powerful. Even on "down" days when you don't feel like it, you can't stop yourself from feeling much better after expressing gratitude and focusing on your goals.

Will you have a bad day every once in awhile? Yes! But with practice and dedication, we're sure your happiness and satisfaction with your life and its components will increase dramatically.

Does this take effort? Yes, it takes intentional thought and practice to turn negatives to positives. To look for the silver lining.

When you try to stop negative thoughts, you are focusing on what you don't want—negative thoughts—and you will attract an abundance of them. They can never disappear if you are focused on them. The "stop" part is irrelevant—the negative thoughts are your focus. It doesn't matter if you are trying to stop negative thoughts or control them or push them away; the result is the same. Your focus is on negative thoughts, and, by the law of attraction, you are inviting more of them to you.

Be intentionally persistent, as you have been programmed to think a certain way. Exactly like planting seeds, as you appreciate, you are planting and transforming your thinking habits that may have been with you for years or decades. It will likely take you between 30—90 days to change a habit, or longer, depending on what you are changing. Start today.

Make it a daily practice to plant good thoughts to *appreciate* all the things in your day. Appreciate your health. That your car gets you where you need to go. For your home, family, work, and friends. For your surroundings, meals, pets, and the penny you found on the ground. That your washing machine works, you have a roof over your head, your socks are intact, and that you can see, hear, taste, touch, feel, and smell. The magnificent beauty of the day. The object is to find *something and someone*—even if minute—for which to be grateful.

Appreciate, compliment, praise, and give thanks for all things. Every time you say "Thank you," it is a good thought! As you plant more and more *good* thoughts, the negative thoughts will be wiped out. Why? Because your focus is on good thoughts, and what you focus on, you attract.

Acknowledge, but don't dwell on negative thoughts. Don't worry about them. If any come, make light of them, shrug them off, and let them be your reminder to deliberately think more good thoughts *now*.

The more appreciating thoughts you can plant in a day, the faster your life will be utterly transformed into all good. If you spend only one day speaking of good things and saying "Thank you" at every single opportunity, you will not believe your tomorrow.

Expressing gratitude and being grateful is a good thing. You'll probably have days you forget, despite your good intentions and excitement, but keep at it!

Another important reason for remaining in a state of appreciation is that when you are in such a state, you are in one of the highest emotional states possible. When your focus is on appreciating what you have received, you will receive more. It becomes an upward-spiraling process of ever-increasing abundance that just keeps getting better and better.

Appreciating yourself builds your self-esteem. It's loving yourself. This might feel a little weird at first, but self–love is a very important part of success.

Think about it. The more grateful people are for the gifts we give them, the more inclined we are to give them more gifts. Their gratitude and appreciation reinforces our giving. The same principle holds true on a universal and spiritual level as it does on an interpersonal one.

Use your words to lift people

We have a number of former students with whom we keep in touch. Recently, we heard from a young woman embarking on her career who is continually disappointed by the lack of support of her parents and significant other. "What do you do when you're all alone and everyone you love is against you?" she asked. "Everyone seems to be mad at me for wanting a future. They tell me I can't do what I want to become. What do I do?"

Words are so incredibly powerful. Do you have a memory of someone in your life you loved or respected who made a comment, even if in jest or teasing, that sticks with you to this day? Kim has one from 5th grade. Her math teacher teased her for being "her little math genius" one night when meeting with her mother. That teacher's judgment on her still affects her confidence and abilities to feel she can understand and perform math well, even though she's proven to be quite capable.

Who has spoken to you?

Our words can damage or heal a person in the short- and long-term. They can make a difference in how that person talks and thinks about themselves the rest of their life. With your words you can lift someone out of depression and help a person become the success they want to become.

You can be the right person for somebody else. You can't be certain what is going on inside a person, but the power of a compliment or an encouraging word can keep a person from giving up on themselves or making a wrong decision.

Does it seem to you to be so easy for people to think bad things and so hard to think good thoughts of themselves? We do this because we have been taught not to be conceited. Remember when you were in school and you told somebody how good you were at something? Did they look at you and say, "You are so stuck on yourself?"

We have been programmed not to tell ourselves that we are good. We are good-looking. We are smart. Every thought that goes unchallenged becomes true. It takes root as a seed and grows as you nurture it. When you give thought water, it grows.

People need encouragement. We need approval. People need to know we believe in them. They need to know they are talented, creative, gifted, and that we appreciate them.

Expressing gratitude and health

Expressing gratitude means expressing thankfulness, counting your blessings, noticing simple pleasures, and acknowledging everything you receive. It means learning to live your life as if everything were a miracle and being aware on a continuous basis of how much you've been given. Expressing gratitude shifts your focus from what your life lacks to the abundance that is already present. In addition, behavioral and psychological research has shown the surprising life improvements that can stem from the practice of expressing gratitude. Giving thanks makes people happier and more resilient. It strengthens relationships, improves health, and reduces stress.

Two researchers found a connection between gratitude and good health. Michael McCollough and Robert Emmons were curious about why people involved in their faith seem to have more happiness and a greater sense of well-being than those who aren't and decided to study the connections. After making initial observations and compiling all the previous research on gratitude, they conducted the *Research Project on Gratitude and Thanksgiving*.

The study, published in the Journal of Personality and Social Psychology, 2003, required several hundred people in three different groups to keep daily diaries. The first group kept a diary of the events that occurred during the day, while the second group recorded their unpleasant experiences. The last group made a daily list of things for which they were grateful.

The results of the study indicated that daily gratitude exercises resulted in higher reported levels of alertness, enthusiasm, determination, optimism, and energy. Additionally, the gratitude group experienced less depression and stress, was more likely to help others, exercised more regularly, and made more progress toward personal goals. According to the findings, people who feel grateful are also more likely to feel loved. McCollough and Emmons also noted that gratitude encouraged a positive cycle of reciprocal kindness among people since one act of gratitude encourages another.

McCullough says these results also seem to show that gratitude works independently of faith. Though gratitude is a substantial part of most religions, he says the benefits extend to the general population, regardless of faith or lack thereof.

In light of his research, McCullough suggests that anyone can increase their sense of well-being and create positive social effects just from counting their blessings.

Whatever else each of us derives from our work, there may be nothing more precious than the feeling that we truly matter—that we contribute unique value to the whole, and that we're recognized for it.

Workers want their managers to be genuinely interested in their well-being. When managers appreciate their workers, it goes much farther than just giving them a raise.

Feeling genuinely appreciated lifts people up. At the most basic level, it makes us feel energized. When our value feels at risk, as it so often does, that worry becomes preoccupying, draining our energy and productivity.

So why is it that openly praising or expressing appreciation to other people easily seems so awkward, uncomfortable, or even disingenuous?

The obvious answer is that we're not fluent in the language or acceptance of positive emotions in our relationships. We're so unaccustomed to sharing them that we don't feel comfortable doing so. Heartfelt appreciation is a muscle we've not spent much time exercising or felt encouraged to build.

We're often more experienced at expressing negative emotions, often without recognizing their negative impact on others until much later, if we do at all.

Catch others Doing WUCA!

Alex Haley, author of *Roots*, lived by these six words: *Find the good and praise it.*

If you have difficulty openly appreciating others, it's likely you also find it difficult to appreciate yourself. Take a few moments at the end of the day to ask yourself this simple question: "What can I feel proud of today?" If you are committed to constant self-improvement, you can also ask yourself, "What could I do better tomorrow?" The answers to both questions hold your value.

Make it a priority to notice what others are doing right. Catch them Doing WUCA! The more you work at it, the better you'll get at it, and the more natural it will become for you. For example, start by thinking about what positive qualities, behaviors, and contributions you currently take for granted among the members of your family or team. Ask yourself what unique contributions each of them bring to the table.

Be appreciative. The more specific you can be about what you value—and the more you notice what's most meaningful—the more positive your impact on that person is likely to be. Handwritten notes make a bigger impression than an e-mail or a passing comment, but better any one of them than nothing at all.

We're all more vulnerable and needy than we like to acknowledge. Authentically appreciating others will make you feel better about yourself. It will also increase the likelihood they'll invest more your relationship. The human instinct for reciprocity runs deep.

Don't overlook what is right in front of you. Appreciate what you have and see the blessing.

Enjoy the Coffee

A group of alumni, highly established in their careers, got together to visit their old university professor. Conversation soon turned into complaints about stress in work and life. Offering his guests coffee, the professor went to the kitchen and returned with a large pot of coffee and an assortment of cups—porcelain, plastic, glass, crystal, some plain-looking, some expensive, some exquisite—telling them to help themselves.

When all the students had a cup of coffee in hand, the professor said:

"If you noticed, all the nice-looking expensive cups were taken up, leaving behind the plain and cheap ones. While it is but normal for you to want only the best for yourselves, that is the source of your problems and stress. Be assured that the cup itself adds no quality to the coffee in most cases, just more expense and, in some cases, even hides what we drink.

"What all of you really wanted was coffee, not the cup, but you consciously went for the best cups and then began eyeing each other's cups.

"Now consider this: Life is the coffee, and the jobs, money and position in society are the cups. They are just tools to hold and contain Life, and the type of cup we have does not define, nor change the quality of Life we live. Sometimes, by concentrating only on the cup, we fail to enjoy the coffee God has provided us. God brews the coffee, not the cups... enjoy your coffee."

Make appreciation a habit and watch your life change.

When you know how important gratitude is for your life, pay it forward.

Send someone a note and make them feel appreciated. Or send out a quick e-mail and let someone you know you care about them or you were just thinking of them. For example, we send out Be WUCA! certificates and Catch Them Doing WUCA! cards to people who demonstrate WUCA!

In addition to contributing and helping your family and friends get more out of their life by being grateful, you will also be able to build a stronger connection with those you love and care about.

Be sure to take all opportunities to appreciate those still in your midst. All too often we wish, "If I only would have told them…"

Write a living eulogy

When you go to a funeral, there is often a chance for people to stand up and tell how much the deceased person meant to them or what they did. It is a story about how wonderful a person they were when they were alive. The sad part of that is the person will likely never have heard all of the wonderful things that were said about them.

Wouldn't it mean more if all of the good that you wanted to tell about that person was told to them while living? Try it. Stop right now and think of someone still alive, someone that if you were asked, you would write a eulogy about them.

A eulogy is a speech or writing in high praise of a person. Write a eulogy of a person whom you appreciate or of a person who has wronged you in some way. This exercise is a way to appreciate others and can also be a way to forgive.

Writing a eulogy is truly an honor. Your words will paint a picture through the memories, anecdotes, and stories you tell.

A eulogy allows others to get to know the person—who they are, what they do, and what they enjoy about life.

The most touching and meaningful eulogies are written from the heart. A eulogy does not have to be perfect. Whatever you write will be appreciated.

Use the following to help you begin. A eulogy may contain:

a condensed life history of the person.

_____

_____

_____

details about family, friends, work/career, interests, and achievements.

_____

_____

_____

favorite memories, poems, songs, quotes, or religious writings.

_____

_____

_____

Think about the person and the relationship you have with them. Where you met (if you are not family), things you do together, humorous or touching memories, and what you would miss the most might be things you decide to share.

_____

_____

_____

Talk with family members and close friends to gather important information. Even co-workers may have valuable things to share. Some important information to include in the eulogy:

Person's age/date of birth/place of birth

_____

_____

_____

Family and other close relationships

_____

_____

_____

Education/work/career

_____

_____

_____

Hobbies or special interests

_____

_____

_____

Places the person lived

_____

_____

_____

Special accomplishments

_____

_____

_____

Some people prefer to prepare a serious eulogy while others will want to keep the tone light. A mix of both elements, solemnity and humor, is usually best. It allows the audience to share in the celebration of a life.

Write in your own voice. That means to write it in the same way you would normally talk. Don't get bogged down by the formalities of writing.

Keep in mind the most important thing: write from your heart.

People that are with you right now at this moment have a purpose for being in front of you. Appreciate every moment you are in and every person that you are with.

Watch for opportunities to lift other people up. When you lift them by appreciating them, you lift yourself up to heights where you have never been before.

A person's heart gravitates toward appreciation and closes the loop in our relationships.

Catch people Doing WUCA!

Express gratitude.

Be appreciative.

TO CREATE A MORE APPRECIATIVE ENVIRONMENT, I WILL:

IN MY BUSINESS

_____

_____

IN MY WORKPLACE

_____

_____

IN MY CHURCH

_____

_____

IN MY FAMILY

_____

_____

IN MY SCHOOL

_____

_____

IN MY COMMUNITY

_____

_____

IN MY ORGANIZATION

_____

_____

Energy Blocks to Living WUCA!

———⊖⊗⊗⊖———

$\mathcal{M}$ ANY OF YOUR SOURCES OF illness and diseases are two different but closely related areas: physiological stress caused by your environment, and internal stress inside of you with your thoughts.

Most of your sicknesses are triggered by your subconscious mind.

Guilt and worry—the evil twins of stress

These two gremlins have a way of blocking positive energy flowing through us.

Times when you are unsure about the future and do not have direction in life can be extremely stressful and wreak physical and emotional havoc on the body, creating energy blocks.

People who harbor guilt and continue to worry over past wrongs often have a difficult time thinking positively or take positive steps to improve their life. They explain their present unhappiness and dissatisfaction with the self-defeating mantra, "I deserve to be unhappy." Somewhere in the back of their minds, they believe happiness won't last for them. They don't deserve it. Why even bother to try?

Feeling guilty can bring feelings of **self-hate**. Of course you don't like yourself. Of course you're depressed. Look what you did! Letting guilt go can be very difficult. Start by taking a serious look at what you did, or *think* you did, and put it into perspective.

Remember, no one can **make** you feel anything. You allow what you feel.

Then there is guilt's twin, worry.

Did you know that 92 percent of the things we worry about never happen? And that 95 percent of our ailments are caused by stress? The way you respond to your environment creates internal stress. With that knowledge, let's think about how to unlearn this behavior and break this negative energy habit.

Begin by putting your worries into two categories: things over which you have some control and things you do not. You need to figure out how to let go of the things over which you have no control. For the things you can influence, form a plan of action that will produce a more positive outcome.

Maybe you feel your concerns are valid and you have a legitimate reason to worry. Maybe you feel your marriage is going poorly and you might end up alone. Maybe someone close to you is dying. Maybe you are worried about serious financial concerns. Kids. Health. Money. The list goes on and on.

If there truly isn't much you can do to change a particular problem's outcome, don't just sit around and complain. Spend your time forming a plan of action—positive planning with a positive mindset—for how you will handle the situation when it occurs. Your action will contribute to the result and your circumstances will not just "happen" to you.

Work with what you have. Make good choices for what you know needs to be done and do it. Above all, keep focused on your vision and actively work toward it.

Worry is the result of too much negative thinking. Change your "what if it does not work?" to "what if I achieve all of my goals?" It takes the same amount of thought process. Work your goals.

Living your passion and purpose keeps you healthy. When you are doing what you love, you get up in the morning doing what you *love* to do, not what you *have* to do. That is a huge mental shift.

The outcome of not doing what you were created to do is undue stress in your life. Stress releases an overabundant amount of the chemical called cortisol, which can have devastating physical effects on your body and your health.

This chart from AARP shows what stress can do to us over time.

Symptoms of stress:

- » Frequent headaches, jaw clenching or pain
- » Gritting or grinding teeth
- » Tremors, or trembling lips and/or hands
- » Neck ache, back pain, or muscle spasms
- » Light-headedness, faintness, or dizziness
- » Ringing, buzzing or "popping sounds"
- » Dry mouth or problems swallowing
- » Frequent colds, infections or cold sores
- » Unexplained or frequent "allergy" attacks
- » Heartburn, stomach pain, or nausea
- » Excess belching or flatulence
- » Constipation or diarrhea
- » Difficulty breathing or sighing
- » Sudden attacks of panic

» Chest pain, or palpitations

» Excess anxiety, worry, guilt, or nervousness

» Increased anger, frustration, or hostility

» Depression, frequent, or wild mood swings

» Increased or decreased appetite

» Insomnia, nightmares, or disturbing dreams

» Difficulty concentrating or racing thoughts

» Forgetfulness, disorganization, or confusion

» Difficulty in making decisions

» Feeling overloaded or overwhelmed

» Frequent crying spells or suicidal thoughts

» Feelings of loneliness or worthlessness

» Little interest in appearance or punctuality

» Increased frustration, irritability, or edginess

» Overreaction to petty annoyances

» Reduced work efficiency or productivity

» Weight gain or loss without dieting

Yikes! Do any of these sound familiar to you? Like us, we bet these are distractions you don't want in your life! By lowering your stressors and relieving your symptoms, discovering your passion and purpose, setting your vision, and establishing your goals to achieve your success, your body will respond with increased health and vitality.

Rid yourself of the voices in your head that bring up past experiences to move toward a positive and healthful future.

Negative voices block positive energy

As we said before, words matter. As people grow up, creativity is often stolen by words that we hear. These negative voices become blocks to positive energy.

Frank relates a story from Gordon Mackenzie's *Orbiting the Giant Hairball*, sharing visits with individual classes of kindergarteners through sixth graders. To each class, he asks, "How many of you like to draw?" You know kindergartners—every one of them is jumping around yelling, "Me! I like to draw and I'm the best draw-er!"

He calls in the first- and second-graders and receives more enthusiastic responses. In the third grade, when he asks, "How many of you like to draw?" they're sitting on the floor and don't jump around. About half of them raise their hand saying they like to draw. To "Who's the best draw-er?" 50 percent of those hands go down and 50 percent stay up.

Up to the sixth-graders. "How many of you like to draw?" Three people raise their hands. "Who's the best draw-er?" Everybody in the sixth grade turns to one person and points.

What Mackenzie surmises is that, as kids go through school, we slap creativity out of them. We say, "Don't doodle, get to your math."

Don't jump around, sit in your seat.

Stay still.

Do what the policy says. Form into my box.

So we make them fit in the giant hairball of our education system, often stifling them. Then, in adulthood, we ask people to think creatively to solve problems and to think outside the box. Does it work? Maybe, but it's likely pretty hard because we have been taught to stay in the box. We don't know any differently. The creative side of us may be buried deep within.

In kindergarten we all liked to draw, to play, to dream! Now if you interact with creative types, are you able to throw in some far-out ideas, or have you been stripped of your kindergarten enthusiasm? How often do you hear, "You can't do that! How can we make that happen?" If these are phrases you hear from yourself, you may want to rethink your words to be supportive.

Sometimes we inhibit ourselves. Think on these questions and see if you are putting up your own roadblocks.

> » What am I saying that is keeping me from succeeding?
> » How am I sabotaging my relationships?
> » What do I do to put myself at risk of failing?
> » What am I saying to miss opportunities for success?

Let's encourage our natural gifts and work to imagine and conjure new ideas.

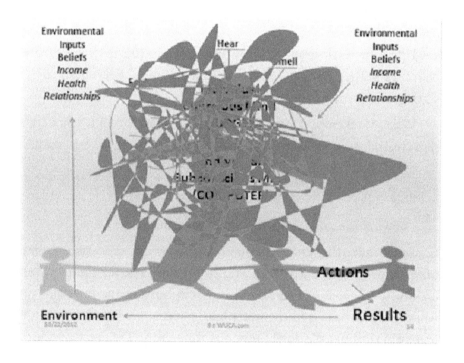

Emotional Freedom Technique (EFT) clears energy blocks

We became acquainted with EFT a few years ago and it's been

very helpful personally and with people we've coached. In fact, Frank controls a condition that had plagued him for years called Restless Leg Syndrome using this method. It's also being used successfully treating people with Post-Traumatic Stress Disorder, PTSD.

The basic premise of the Emotional Freedom Techniques is that the cause of all negative emotions is a disruption in the body's energy system. Many people call this technique *tapping* because that's what you do. You literally tap with your fingertips on body points to relieve stress.

When our energy is flowing normally, without obstruction, we feel good in every way. When our energy becomes blocked or stagnant or is otherwise disrupted along one or more of the body's energy meridians, negative or damaging emotions can develop along with all types of physical symptoms. This idea has been the centerpiece of Eastern medicine for thousands of years.

Sometimes the improvement is permanent, while in other cases the process needs to be continued. But even if symptoms return, they can usually be reduced or eliminated quickly and effectively just by repeating the procedure.

People are often astonished at the results they experience because their belief systems have not yet adapted to this commonsense process. The treatment of physical, emotional, and performance issues is supposed to be much more difficult than simply tapping with your fingertips on key acupuncture points.

The EFT basics are extremely easy to use. Small children learn it quickly, and kids as young as eight or 10 have no trouble teaching it to others. It's fully portable, requires no special equipment, can be used at any time of the day or night, under any circumstances, and it's completely free.

No drugs, surgeries, radiations, or other medical interventions are involved in EFT. In fact, it's so different from conventional medicine that the medical profession often has difficulty explaining its results.

There is an entire international community who uses tapping to relieve stress.

You can tap on which side of your body is most comfortable for you. There really is no "wrong" place to tap. The goal is to verbalize and eliminate negative energy and assure yourself that you believe in, love, and accept yourself for who you are.

A brief explanation

1. Identify your issue. For example, let's say you're super-stressed with test anxiety.

2. Identify the level of your stress on a scale from one to 10— with one at the lowest level. Give it a number.

3. Using two or three fingers, tap on the "karate chop" point on the soft outside pad of your hand to set up your issue.

4. As you tap on this karate chop point, phrase words to describe what you are feeling. Something like this will do: "Even though I am scared that I have to take this test, I still love and accept myself." Repeat this phrase, tapping all the while, about 6—10 times.

5. Now you'll make a round of your body's acupuncture points and use tapping's acupressure to release the energy. Following the diagram, start at the inside edge of your eye, tapping about a half-dozen times per spot. As you tap, vocalize whatever you are feeling."

6. Proceed to the outside eye, under your nose, chin, collarbone, under your arm, and top of your head.

7. Do about 3—5 rounds of these points, saying the same phrase or a variation, "I worry that I'm not prepared for this test," "Even though I hate having to take tests…" "Even though I'm never any good at tests—I always fail them…" etc.

8. Take a breath through your nose and slowly release it.

9. Check your stress level. If it is still high, then have another session. If you've dropped to a low number, you've released your pent-up negative energy and should feel notably better.

A good source for more information that we always recommend is www.TheTappingSolution.com.

WUCA! Dude's Tapping Points

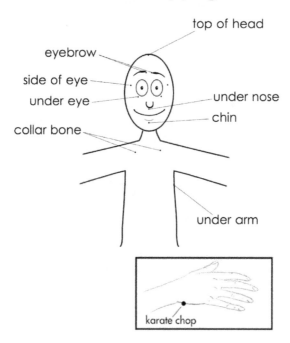

No technique or procedure works for everyone but by all accounts the vast majority of those who try EFT for a specific problem experience significant improvement. It makes sense that if your energy is balanced, everything inside and around you benefits.

People are using EFT successfully with veterans with PTSD and with people who have experienced traumatic violent events, as in Rwanda and mass shootings in schools.

There are stunning results through tapping that compare

favorably with prescription drugs, surgical procedures, and other medical treatments. We encourage practitioners and newcomers alike to experiment—to try it on everything from weight loss to stopping smoking to finances to healing from abuse to body image. You can tap on absolutely everything that stresses you in your life.

Try it!

WUCA! In Action

WUCA! in Action

Putting the pieces together

THE PRINCIPLES TO BE WUCA! can be applied in any personal, business, or organizational relationship.

In the following pages, we highlight some specific places to implement WUCA!

If you'd like to see how WUCA! coaching can create a WUCA! environment for your family, community, or workplace to give you a WUCA! competitive advantage, we'd love to hear from you and see how we can help you transform and accomplish great relationships. It will be the best investment for your growth.

Set a Be WUCA! environment for student success:

Coaching in the Classroom

Note: if you haven't spent any time in a school lately, volunteer any amount of time you can. Once you've been on the inside and learned the environment, you

*are guaranteed to gain tremendous appreciation for our
teachers and administrators and the challenges they face
each and every single day. Thank them. Profusely.*

Our experiences hiring high school and young adult workers
chime in with the frustration of other business owners and heads of
corporations: the quality of worker coming out of the high schools is
not up to standard. Workers need to show up on time and be ready
to work. They need to be able to get along and work well with others.
There is often an air of entitlement with younger employees. They
think that their mere presence is a gift to the business without hard
work. So we took the requests for a stronger worker to the classroom
to see if WUCA! would make a difference.

Coaching in the Classroom (CIC) was created and began as a pilot
project in 2009, focusing on 7th—12th-graders in a rural Iowa school
district and a metro alternative school, capitalizing on our more than
25 years' expertise in rural business and economic development. CIC
identifies student's passions, and uses positive self-talk and goal-
setting utilized by championship athletes to develop championship
students in the classroom.

CIC morphed after its first year in the rural district into a
process that addresses students' behaviors that put them "at-risk"
of not graduating on time with their class, as defined by the Iowa
Department of Education. The four criteria are:

- » not being proficient in numeracy and literacy on Iowa
  Assessments;
- » failing at least one class;
- » not participating in any school activity; and
- » poor attendance and/or habitual tardiness.

If a student has a "check" in two of the four categories, they are
considered "at-risk." This designation doesn't mean the child has

substance abuse problems, any mental deficiencies, or other issues that could label them "at-risk." It simply means that these behaviors are red flags—indicators that a student is developing habits that aren't good for their academic and personal success in life.

Recognizing that these students will likely remain in their communities as employees and business owners after graduation, CIC connects these "at-risk" criteria to the behaviors employers require in employees that impact a workforce: show up on time. Be a lifelong learner and remember your lessons. Participate with others. Do "A"-quality work and turn it in on time.

The reality of our classrooms today is that our students are being taught core fundamentals, but our educational system, government mandates, and lack of solid parenting don't allow time or staff to help them bridge the gap between school learning and applicability to the workforce once they leave school.

Coaching in the Classroom believes that all students will succeed when their passions, purpose, and goals align with their personal and occupational visions. CIC seeks to be the bridge that keeps all students in school through graduation and encourages self-motivation and drive for success in today's global workforce. CIC goals are to:

» improve scores of standardized assessments and other examinations.

» instill entrepreneurial spirit and skills to help students see the possibility of being local business owners and leaders.

» strengthen the local workforce by reinforcing the relevance of classroom instruction material to their futures.

» improve self-esteem of students when they achieve personal success raising scores and feel more hopeful about their future options.

» experience positive movement from students on youth surveys that measure students' sense of security, belonging, and other less tangible but extremely important indicators for success.

» improve behavior of students in the community.

» improve relationships between students, staff, and faculty in school.

» improve relationships between the school, students, and the community.

Due to many factors, rural communities are being forced to look for new ways to sustain their towns and school districts. In this ever-evolving environment, the area workforce is changing from a blend of white- and blue-collar workers to a more dominant blue collar workforce, often resulting in more college-educated children choosing to look in metropolitan areas for work. The students who remain in their home area are more likely students for whom school was a more challenging and less satisfying experience. These are the fine, bright people who, sooner or later, will likely become mayors and run the communities, city councils, school boards, churches, and civic organizations, owning businesses within the community.

In addition to in-class presentations, discussions, and field trips, CIC can specifically link students with businesses of interest to their identified passions. Communities, especially those in rural areas, need to aggressively integrate these students to pursue business succession and workforce improvement strategies in the area to increase population and school enrollment.

CIC includes real-life stories about roles and expectations as employees compared to how their employers view them. For example, students learn that tattoos, piercings, and texting on the job they feel are personal expressions and rights can affect their hirability and longevity at a business.

We set in place individual academic, extracurricular, and work-related steps to identify how to make life vision become reality.

Sometimes this includes self-reflection and that is really, really tough for this population of students. Heck, most people don't reflect because we often don't like what we see, but it's necessary for growth. It's a valuable tool. So we include exercises that require them to glimpse into themselves and what they want. We encourage that they deserve what they dream. And that often requires changing their behaviors.

Involvement of the local businesses to strengthen the workforce can take place through relevant speakers to the classes, identifying gaps in businesses needed by the community, how students can look to fill the gaps, and understand how their high school learning will impact their future goals. It also takes the community to want to reach out to the students to welcome, engage, and recognize the talents they have to offer. Plus, community members need enthusiasm and patience to teach students the skills they need to learn.

In addition to all the activities and exercises included in CIC, we have encouraged students by

» telling them the criteria by which they have been measured since kindergarten. The mere knowledge of this "list" has been a revelation.

» telling them how to get off "the list" and that the ability to do so is completely within their power.

» helping them understand that their school attendance, classroom performance, attitude, and how they apply themselves at school matters to their ability to graduate and to future employment.

» ending every single class, and calling often through the halls, the single most important message from *Coaching in the Classroom*: **make good choices.**

It hasn't made us popular, but we're known for it!

Results

> » Within months of CIC's inception, the number of students sent to the principal's office for misbehavior was down more than 50 percent.

> » Students recognize that classroom work in core areas has direct impact on their future either in further education, enlisting in the military, or by remaining in or near their hometown and joining the workforce.

> » Student population considered "at-risk" has decreased from 41 to 12.3 percent.

By identifying passions and aspirations with all students early in their school careers and helping them determine the steps to make their goals reality, students are more focused, better-behaved, and satisfied in high school, and better prepared whether they pursue a military career, go to college, or join the workforce upon graduation.

The following is an example of a lesson.

CIC promotes "School is your job" to students.

Dear Students: News flash: school is your job. When you are in school getting any diploma or degree, your attitude should reflect: "This is my job."

While you're rolling that concept around your gray matter, here are four parts of school that relate to your efforts with what a job would require of you: classes, grades, attendance, and participation.

Classes—Your classes are your job description. They are why you are there and what you need to learn to get to where you want to go. It is up to you to do the work as it is required by your employer (teacher/instructor) in the timeframe that is assigned. You have been given an assignment, direction, and deadline. Now go do it!

Grades—Your grades are your employee review and evaluation. It is how well you are doing the job you were hired to do. Do you get it done with just the minimal amount of effort or do you go above and beyond? If you get a "C" and are just doing average work, expect the average increase in wages. But if you go above the average and get a "B" or an "A," you might be in line for a larger raise and/or even a promotion. Employers are looking for people who will do more than just the required amount of work.

Attendance –Do you skip school because you're too tired? Just don't feel like going and stay snoozing in bed? Let's say you're at school every day. Are you in your seat on time, ready to learn, for each class? Being present and on time ready to work when you are supposed to is an extremely important consideration because employers count on their workers being where they are supposed to be when they are supposed to be there. When an employee does not show up, the employer cannot serve their customer in the proper way. Plus, it is just plain common courtesy and consideration of other people to fulfill an expectation that you will be where and when you promised.

Extracurricular activities—Employers need to have employees who work well with others because all kinds of people from different backgrounds and experiences will be in the workforce and the business runs on teamwork. The employee is expected to work in concert with and contribute as a productive member of the business to produce a product. When you do not learn how to play well with others, you are passed over for opportunities to grow in the company and increase your income. So be in a play. Try out your smarts in debate, join a speech or photography club or toot your horn in band. Start an entrepreneurship club, build apps for smart phones, go out for a sport, or be a cheerleader. If your school doesn't have what interests you, start something! The relationships you will build and the ability to play well with others will serve you in and out of school. And just may earn you more money.

That said, money should not be the driver of your efforts. Work ethic is how well you do what you were asked to do and the attitude you bring to the job without considering pay. If you want to be recognized for your hard work, work as though it would not matter if you were paid well or not.

These four areas of your education will be part of your life forever. You will always be evaluated on what work you are supposed to do, how well you do it, whether you are timely and prompt, and if you get along well with your co-workers and customers. Whether you own your own business or work for someone else in a private business, a non-profit organization, or a government entity, you are evaluated by others on how well and ethically you do the work you are paid to do.

Next time you think school doesn't relate to the "real world," think again.

Brittany's story: A change in attitude yields a future

We met Brittany as a sophomore in 2008 when we began teaching *Coaching in the Classroom.*

A young woman from a hard-working family facing some challenges, Brittany, in this phase of her life, was a free spirit in search of herself. Not following any one "look," she colored her hair and wore a variety of clothing to express herself. Academically, she had passed few classes and accumulated few credits toward graduation. Her future looked pretty dim unless she made changes in her life.

We could see she was smart. Very smart. Capable. Very kind to a great many people, especially those she let into her trust. What she lacked was belief in herself and a support system to encourage her intelligence and skills. Her circle of friends tended to be students from similar backgrounds for mutual support—and not always good choices.

During the course of the next three years, we worked closely with Brittany at school, on Facebook, in phone conversations, and many, many texts. We talked through drama. We talked through friendships and how associations affect a person and their decisions. We talked about her family and what she was dealing with at home. We advised her what we told the classes—that sometimes you have to leave behind the life you know to have the life you want. Sometimes figuratively. Sometimes literally.

As her time with us progressed and she matured, Brittany heard the message of WUCA!

She shifted her shocking hair colors in favor of highlighting to bright shades to show her individuality.

She heard and chose the message of C + A = R.

She heard the message of understanding the viewpoints of others, asking bright, thoughtful, curious, intuitive questions.

She heard the message of identifying her passions and setting goals.

She heard the message of changing the way she looks at life.

Most importantly, she chose to act on what she heard.

Through extremely hard work, dedication, taking extra classes, getting extra help from teachers, choosing different friends or, a lot of time, choosing to be alone, Brittany chose to turn around her circumstances and act differently to gain the result she desired.

She was one of 12 high school students to participate in a deliberative dialogue on *America's Role in the World*, mentioned earlier in this book. Her comments were included in a report and video shared at the 50th anniversary of the Dartmouth Conference on U.S./Russia relations in 2010 in Washington, D.C.

She graduated on time, with her class. We were there to celebrate with her and her family. And we're still celebrating.

Now in her early 20s, Brittany has gone on to college—the first in her family to do so. And she has a 3.5 GPA.

That's choosing your direction.

That's leaving the past to press on to the future.

That's realizing your value.

That's a star.

That's the power of WUCA!

WUCA! actions to grow local businesses and school populations

During the course of the last several years, we have noticed differences about the adults in our personal and professional lives: the young adults think differently than we do. In ours and previous generations, the business attitude has often been quite self-centered with a mindset, "I succeeded on my own. Nobody helped me. Why should I help anyone else?"

Today's young adults are connected, perhaps nudged or propelled by social media and sharing from music to homework to business, and they like it. It's our observation that their view is to want everybody and everything to succeed. The more, the merrier. If you win, I win. Instead of working in silos and cubbies, they want to have open-space offices, technology, and platform sharing that enables the whole to succeed in faster time than individually. They also appear to be happier doing so.

Excitingly, we believe our economy requires this type of collaboration. Which means knowing how to build relationships. It means finding a common community with clearly-identified passion, purpose, vision, and goals.

Leadership thinking requires changing how you view the world. The collaborators may need to change the way they look at the world so the things they look at change. This change of thinking may require the community to shift its view and thinking, as well.

When you change the
way you look at things,
the things you
look at change.

If growth is a desire of the community, it needs to live WUCA!, welcoming and accepting new people and new ideas.

Here are important WUCA! actions for community leaders to change their circumstances that result in growing civil communities with young people:

1. Lead from a WUCA! perspective.

    a. Welcome and attract others through your attitude.

    b. Understand and actively listen. Be respectful and honor the beliefs of others.

    c. Comfort, discover, and nurture others' passions, purpose, vision, and goals.

    d. Appreciate, trust, and express gratitude to and for others.

2. Recognize the value of dialogue and deliberation and how they motivate individuals to participate and support the direction of the community.

3. Foster a community spirit of entrepreneurship that develops and coaches entrepreneurs.

4. Identify and connect community and organizational assets.

Just as we have talked throughout this book, communities, too, become what they think about. The mind and attitude of the community is determined by its citizens and its leaders. The community is what it is, who it is, and where it is because of what has gone into its mind since it began. So if you want your community to change the direction it is going, it needs to change who it is and what it is and that will only happen when it decides to change what goes into its mind.

Encourage youth involvement

At a time when many people feel overwhelmed by the problems and challenges facing children and adolescents, communities across the country can discover new energy by working together to increase civility toward a positive vision for people and the community's future.

Instead of focusing only on problems of young people, successful, forward-thinking communities unite to nurture the positive development of youth to build a strong, supportive foundation based on civility.

Much like playing in a jazz ensemble, each musician (community member) must know the tune and listen to the other members. All players must improvise together—sometimes taking the lead and sometimes blending into the background. To create a community-wide commitment to youth, all the "players" need to be an ensemble working toward a common vision of what is needed to promote the healthy development of young people and their role in the community.

Healthy Be WUCA! communities that build civility and family-friendly supports ensure:

» all residents take personal responsibility for efforts to build civility in relationships.

» the community thinks and acts inter-generationally.

» all children and teenagers frequently have opportunity to be in service to others.

» families are supported, educated, and equipped.

» all children and teenagers receive support in informal settings and in places where youth gather.

» neighborhoods and schools are places of caring, support, and safety.

» schools mobilize to promote caring, clear boundaries, and sustained relationships with adults.

» businesses establish family-friendly policies for all employees.

» virtually all 10-to-18 year-olds are involved in one or more clubs, teams, or other youth-serving organizations that promote community-building as a central part of their mission.

» the media (print, radio, television, social) repeatedly communicate the community's vision, support local mobilization efforts, and provide forums for sharing innovative actions taken by individuals and organizations.

» youth have opportunities to serve, lead, and make decisions in community, government, and service organizations.

» religious institutions mobilize their resources to build civility within their own programs and in the community.

Wouldn't you want to live in a community that welcomes, embraces, and engages youth?

Communities utilizing these Be WUCA! strategies will stem their population decline, attract new families, and integrate their high school students who wish to remain upon graduation to live, raise their families, and become leaders in area businesses.

Conclusion

Conclusion

It's all about making a difference in the world

Are you living WUCA!?

THROUGHOUT OUR BE WUCA! BOOK, we've shared that thoughts become feelings that transform into behaviors, and these behaviors create actions that become your results.

We become what we think about.

Good thoughts become good actions that create good results.

Great thoughts become great actions that create great results.

You and I are responsible for our lives. Every second of every day, we choose how to drive our Be WUCA! CAR. We choose how to be. We choose to accept responsibility for our circumstances. If we don't like our circumstances, we create the vision of the future that we like and then we ACT to attain the results we desire.

Our environment is a mirror of our attitudes and experiences. If we feel that our environment could stand some improvement, we can only bring about that change for the better by improving our attitude. Our outside environment will change when, and only when, we change the environment inside of us.

Everything in the world we want to do or get done, we must do with and through people. Every dollar we will ever earn must come from people. The person we love, and with whom we want to spend the rest of our life, is a human being with whom we must interact. Our children are individuals, each different from any other person who ever lived. In the workplace, treat your co-workers, employees, and boss the way you want to be treated. The common denominator in all relationships is our attitude. The lovingkindness people see and feel whenever we are around.

If you begin to develop and maintain a WUCA attitude to life and the world, you'll be astonished at the changes you'll see.

Treat every person with whom you come in contact as the most important person on Earth. There is nothing in the world that men, women, and children want and need more than self-esteem. They want to be the most important person that you have ever met.

Be the power to feel great about yourself.

Be wise. Help yourself and someone else create the future.

Be a person today to lift others by what you say or how you treat others.

Be free with compliments.

We appreciate you!

Appreciation is limitless, as the person who once quipped, "I am thinking how nice it is that wrinkles don't hurt!"

We are grateful for each other, for all of our family, our children, grandchildren, where we live, our friends, and the great people with whom we get to work every single day. We are eternally grateful that we are blessed to openly worship a great God we know loves us.

We are grateful you chose to read this book. We pray that you put its concepts into practice and that you tell others Being WUCA! are life-changing actions to get along with everyone.

We are grateful to have figured out that when you Be WUCA! to yourself and to others, they will Be WUCA! to you.

Be welcoming.

Be understanding.

Be comfortable and comforting.

Be appreciative.

Be WUCA!

Together, we will change the world.

About the Authors

Frank and Kimberlee Spillers are co-owners of Global Horizons. They provide, create, and teach innovative processes that bring the best out of people to successfully move forward. Their work ranges from political campaigns, legislative issues, national non-profits, to Main Street mom and pop businesses that fuel local economies, families, and communities.

Drawing on more than 25 years of experience from local chamber director to the Director of the Office of Community Development for USDA Rural Development—Iowa to entrepreneur, Frank's expertise has impacted thousands across the U.S. His lifelong passion has been to teach, coach, and encourage people in communities, businesses, and educational settings. Degreed from Chadron State College in Nebraska in secondary business education and psychology, he's also experienced in mediation, dialogue, deliberation, and facilitation in local, state, and federal government and private sectors.

Kim is a Cyclone from Iowa State University in Ames, Iowa, degreed in journalism and public relations, with a broad perspective gained from a lifetime of community leadership. She has served as an editor, member/chair of numerous local, county, regional, and state boards and organizations, been a community organizer, mentor, and business owner, and brings this wide range of experience to her relationships and writing.

The couple lives in a century-plus home in Atlantic, Iowa, traveling to enjoy their grown children and grandbabies. When home, they enjoy a panoramic view of wildlife in the back meadow: deer, groundhogs, coons, possum, and the occasional skunk. In the basement. But not since fox have moved into the neighborhood. Connect with them at www.bewuca.com

Credits/Resources

Books

Canfield, Jack. *The Success Principle.* Collins: An Imprint of HarperCollins Publishers, 2005
Covey, Stephen. *The Seven Habits of Highly Effective People.* Free Press, 1989
Dr. Dr. Wayne Dyer. *The Power of Intention* DVD. Hay House, 2004
Gordon MacKenzie, *Orbiting the Giant Hairball,* Viking, The Penguin Group, a member of Penguin Putnam, Inc.1998
Marianne Williamson, *A Return to Love.* Harper Collins, 1992

Articles

Michael McCollough, Emmons Robert, "Research Project on Gratitude and Thanksgiving," *Journal of Personality and Social Psychology* (2003):

Organizations

Emotional Freedom Techniques www.TheTappingSolution.com.
Kettering Foundation www.kettering.org
National Coalition for Dialogue and Deliberation www.ncdd.org

CPSIA information can be obtained
at www.ICGtesting.com
Printed in the USA
FFHW020636150119
50176789-55103FF

9 781452 569079